D1078854

(19) £3

Starting your own Gardening Business

If you want to know how...

Your Own Business
The complete guide to succeeding with a small business

Book-keeping & Accounting for the Small Business
How to keep the books and maintain financial control over your business

Starting Your Own Business
How to plan, build and manage a successful enterprise

The Ultimate Business Plan
Secure financial backing and support for a successful business

howtobooks

Please send for a free copy of the latest catalogue:

How To Books
3 Newtec Place, Magdalen Road,
Oxford OX4 1RE, United Kingdom
email: info@howtobooks.co.uk
http://www.howtobooks.co.uk

Starting your own Gardening Business

An **Insider Guide** to setting yourself up as a professional gardener

Paul Power

SUCCESSFUL BUSINESS START-UPS

howtobooks

This book is dedicated to the memory of my mother, Mary Power

Published by How To Books Ltd
3 Newtec Place, Magdalen Road
Oxford OX4 1RE, United Kingdom
Tel: (01865) 793806 Fax: (01865) 248780
info@howtobooks.co.uk
www.howtobooks.co.uk

First published 2003
Reprinted 2004

All rights reserved. No part of this work may be reproduced or stored in an information retrieval system (other than for purposes of review) without the express permission of the publisher in writing.

© Copyright 2003 Paul Power

British Library Cataloguing in Publication Data.
A catalogue record for this book is available from the British Library.

Edited by Diana Brueton
Cover design by Baseline Arts Ltd, Oxford
Produced for How To Books by Deer Park Productions
Typeset by PDQ Typesetting, Newcastle-under-Lyme, Staffs.
Printed and bound in Great Britain by Bell & Bain Ltd, Glasgow

NOTE: The material contained in this book is set out in good faith for general guidance and no liability can be accepted for loss or expense incurred as a result of relying in particular circumstances on statements made in the book. Laws and regulations are complex and liable to change, and readers should check the current position with the relevant authorities before making personal arrangements.

Contents

Preface   ix
Acknowledgements   xi

1 A Growing Opportunity   1
Why start a gardening business?   1
Who will want your services?   5
Your skills and aptitudes   7
Have you got what it takes?   10
How much time will your business need?   13
Finding your niche   15
Carrying out some initial market research   17
Summary   19

2 Essential Planning for You and Your Business   20
The importance of business planning   20
Planning a strategy   23
Writing your business plan   25
Detailing your business idea   28
Preparing an initial cash flow forecast   35
Preparing a profit and loss forecast   40
Contingency planning   43
Is your idea viable?   47
Summary   49

3 What's Involved in Starting and Running a Gardening Round?   51
Knowing what you're letting yourself in for   51
Working out the costs of providing your service   53
Getting started   59
Coping with the paperwork   60
Limitations of a gardening round   69
Summary   70

4 The General Gardening Business   72
The inner workings of a general gardening business   72
Some services offered by a general gardening business   73
Getting started   78
Tools   79

Vehicles 84
Financing your business 87
Getting the business – quotes and estimates 90
Some other issues 99
Summary 104

5 Seasonal Opportunities **106**
The benefit of spin-offs 106
You can specialise 107
Lawn-cutting service 108
Build-it and fix-it service 111
Mobile plant nursery 114
Gardening coaching service 116
Always something to do in a garden 119
Summary 120

6 Launching Your Business **121**
Preparing for growth 121
Creating the right image 129
Standing out from the crowd 135
Business stationery 137
Bank accounts 140
Getting your first customers – the gardening round 143
Launching strategy for other businesses 149
Summary 157

7 Bookkeeping and Administration Systems **159**
Tax for the self-employed 159
Value Added Tax 162
Bookkeeping – the options 164
Completing your annual tax return 169
Getting paid every time and on time 169
Staffing issues 173
Summary 176

8 The Gardening Calendar **177**
A year in the gardening business 177
January 178
February 180
March 181

April	182
May	183
June	185
July	186
August	187
September	188
October	189
November	190
December	191
Summary	193

9 Avoiding Seasonal Blues **194**
When things don't always go to plan	194
Factors outside your control	197
Difficult people and situations	202
Handling complaints	203
Motivation – keeping going	207
Building your knowledge	210
Successful selling	213

Help Directory **221**

Index **225**

Preface

Most of us at some time in our lives hanker after a better lifestyle. To be able to say goodbye to a dreary existence, horrendous commuting, traffic jams, unsympathetic bosses, performance related pay and annual appraisals. Nothing is worse than spending a large proportion of your life working somewhere that you don't enjoy. Lots of people would love to run their own businesses, but all sorts of things stop them from fulfilling their ambitions. As soon as we think of those awful bills that fall unfailingly through our letterboxes, our enthusiasm for going it alone is dampened. The thought of not having a regular salary on which to rely is enough to make an awful existence seem bearable.

I believe this need not be the case. Work should be something you enjoy. Starting and running your own gardening business is an ideal way of escaping the rat race and enjoying a profitable and enormously satisfying career. Whatever your aspirations, be they simply to sell a selection of homegrown plants from your car boot once a month to help pay your bills, or to establish a profitable, all year-round general gardening business, then this book will show you how. All you have to do is have the enthusiasm necessary to take responsibility for your own future and desire more than just having a job. You'll also need to want to run your own business. Believe me, these are two very different things.

You don't need pots of money to start. In fact, your only initial investment will be this book. But what you will need is a willingness to learn and above all to really want to go out there and enjoy what you're doing. My business delivers on each one of my three business and personal goals, which are – fun, profit and freedom. Without these, I believe you don't have a business. You have a job!

Good luck.

Paul Power

Acknowledgements

I am particularly indebted to Nikki Read at How To Books without whose invaluable advice, encouragement and support this project would never have been possible.

My father, the greatest gardener I know, for sharing with me his love of gardening and encouraging me to follow my dreams.

Vivien Wright and Brian Crowe for their unfailing encouragement in getting me from the garden to the desk to write by way of gentle reminders and timely telephone calls. Peter Wright for sharing with me his enormous gardening knowledge and helpful advice.

Diana Brueton for all her hard work in helping prepare the final manuscript and her patience while I fussed and fumbled my way through text and software applications.

To you all, and to everybody who has contributed to publishing this manuscript – a huge thank you.

CHAPTER ONE

A Growing Opportunity

Why start a gardening business?

1. Gardening is big business

Some facts and figures. Gardening has become big business. It's estimated that £3.52 billion is spent annually on gardens in the United Kingdom and this figure is expected to grow every year.

In recent years, gardening has undergone a radical makeover, especially when it comes to the way it is portrayed on our televisions screens. TV gardeners are now enjoying the sort of celebrity status that was previously reserved only for pop stars.

Gone is the image of the traditional flat-capped gardener who advised caution when deciding when to plant runner beans and leeks. Instead, gardening presenters now talk of wonderfully exotic plants with names that intoxicate and aromas that uplift our spirits and carry us off to far flung shores.

Our screens play host to lots of imaginative, bold, talented gardeners and garden designers who have managed to breathe a new life into something that was previously viewed by many as boring.

Today, it seems that almost everyone has an interest in gardening. Even if all you have is a window box hanging optimistically outside your flat, you can find a magazine feature or a television programme that inspires you to create something truly beautiful.

No longer are our homes confined to four brick walls. Now we have outside rooms in our gardens, places where we can relax away the stresses of hectic lifestyles, spaces that we can call our own and make as individual as we are by choosing planting schemes that were previously unheard of. Unimaginatively long, tedious borders have been replaced with waltzing edges and paths that lead to hidden water features, arbours, pergolas, secret gardens and places that are truly magical.

This is gardening at its best.

Yet despite our enthusiasm for having and enjoying these gardens a surprising 76% of the population see gardening as a chore. *This represents enormous potential for anyone who likes gardening to make a successful business from it.*

The freedom of running your own business

Most of us live our lives around our jobs. Everything from the schools we choose for our children to where we holiday every year revolves around our work. Much as we would like to deny it, we are slaves to our occupations: jobs that very often offer little in terms of satisfaction and flexibility.

Many of us dream of setting up our own business, but are daunted by the prospect of being solely responsible for generating our own income.

- How will we cope?
- Who will pay those bills that fall with unfailing regularity on our doormats every week, every month?
- How do we start a business with nothing? Surely any successful venture will need oodles of capital, money that we just haven't got?

Sadly our enthusiasm for breaking out and doing our own thing is overtaken by fear and uncertainty for our futures. The only decision we're capable of making is to do nothing, to stay as we are: suffering poor working conditions, intolerable commutes, cancelled trains, endless targets and a job that leaves us exhausted and stressed. Why? Because we crave the security that a regular monthly salary brings, and the peace of mind that we'll able to pay our bills month in, year out until we retire.

Why I started my own gardening business

Having spent most of my life working for someone else, at 36 years of age I felt I was going nowhere. For whatever reasons my career hadn't advanced as I would have liked it to. I had grown disillusioned with the office politics and bureaucracy that dominated my working days. I was determined to finally take control of my career and make things happen for me as opposed to trying to convince others to include me in their plans.

The only way to do this was for me to employ myself. But what was I going to do?

The first thing I did was make a list of all my skills, followed by my likes and dislikes. Someone once said that the best way to find which business you should start is to first find something you enjoy doing, then find a way to make a living from it. There were three things on my list that I really enjoyed. But at the top, far ahead of the rest, was gardening. I really liked gardening. Now all I had to do was find a way to make it pay.

I started investigating how to go about setting up a gardening business. There was little available in terms of books or references. So I turned to business opportunity magazines and found what I was looking for. Gardening businesses were being offered as franchises. But even if I'd had the enormous amount of money required to buy one, would I really be running my own business, or would I be buying a job in someone else's?

The idea of running my own business appealed to me more than working to the strict guidelines of a franchise agreement and having to pay franchise fees to head office on every weed I pulled. My ambitions went beyond pre-printed agreements, set pricing, royalties, a customer service instruction manual. I wanted to create the best gardening service I could in my own locality. So this is what I set about doing.

This is a business where everything is possible

If the only gardening skill you have is to be able to cut a lawn, but cut it well and take pride in your work, then you have the basis on which to build a successful business. But if you are a keen gardener, skilled, knowledgeable, a master of your craft, then the world outside your door really is waiting for your services. For skilled gardeners are rarities. Sadly, while we now have an abundance of plants and shrubs that were previously unheard of, those willing and capable of looking after them are not so readily available.

There will always be a need for professional gardeners in this country. Whether this is to design, create, build, maintain, prune, advise, or coach novice gardeners in the craft of gardening, there is literally no limit to where this business can take you.

From now on you can enjoy the freedom of working for yourself while enjoying the great outdoors and doing something that is both worthwhile and highly sought after.

> **Surely there is no better way to earn a living?**

My aim in writing this book

This book is written for everyone who wants to have their own gardening business, but is unsure of how to get started and achieve success.

I'm writing not as a business expert but as someone who has set up their business from scratch and has made it a huge success, far exceeding my initial expectations. I earn my living from landscape gardening. It not only pays my bills and keeps me alive, but it also brings enormous satisfaction. My enjoyment and peace of mind comes from knowing that I can support myself and enjoy the independence that running your own business brings. I live my dreams in the present, not the future.

Being self-employed is not for everyone. There are enormous challenges, problems and worries that go with this lifestyle. But if you've got an entrepreneurial spirit and a desire to succeed, then no matter what obstacles your business faces, somehow you can pull through. *You must however, believe in yourself.* I hope that this book answers many of your questions. And I hope that you can use this knowledge to your advantage and fulfil your dreams and ambitions, today. Not tomorrow. For tomorrow may never come. Today is where it's all happening!

Part-time or full-time?

It doesn't matter if you want to work part-time, full-time or run your business alongside your current job, gardening offers as much potential as it does flexibility. While there's no business in the world that is completely fail-safe, the concept of being paid for gardening is not new. It's been tried and tested for centuries. Gardens do their own thing regardless of recession, depression or whatever. Without our intervention gardens quickly become unruly, overgrown and even dangerous. So our world is full of opportunity.

Make your lifestyle your living – enjoy the freedom it brings. See uncertainty as something positive and remember that the greatest thing about working for yourself is that the only person who can make you redundant is you.

My hope is that within these pages you will find answers to the questions that bother you. Take inspiration from the stories. But above all learn as I did that there's no right or wrong way. Running a business is not a 9-to-5 job. It's not something that you begin on a Monday morning and forget on Friday. *It's more than that. It's a way of life.* But if you're not careful it can become your life.

In writing this book, I have provided a framework on which to base your new venture. Gardening businesses will differ depending on where in the country you live, whether you aim to work part-time, full-time, seasonal, or year-round, and on your gardening skills and knowledge, but the problems we all face are the same.

◆ How much will it cost to set up your business?
◆ Where will you find your customers?

- How much should you charge?
- How can you survive throughout the winter?
- What about employing staff?

And all the other questions that might make you worry and prevent you from getting started.

Who will want your services?

The two main markets

- domestic
- commercial.

There are two distinct markets, **domestic** and **commercial**. While recognising that the smaller gardening business can tackle commercial markets, this book is primarily aimed at the domestic market because that is where the greatest opportunity lies.

Domestic market. Operating in this market, your customers don't even have to have their own gardens to require your services. Anyone with even a few flowerpots arranged on the smallest of patios, or a solitary window box, is a potential customer. I get a constant stream of calls from people asking me if I could come and plant up a window box, or create an arrangement of seasonal bedding, or bulbs in some pots and tubs they have dotted around their front doors and patios. While jobs like these may seem unusually small, this does not mean that they cannot be made profitable. And for those people who actually have gardens, whether they be large or small, they will always have a need for your services even if it's just to cut their lawns or water their plants while they're on holiday. Some of the tasks that you may be asked to do will include:

- clearing an overgrown garden, or area of a garden
- cutting a lawn
- trimming and re-shaping a hedge
- carrying out an annual pruning session
- visiting once weekly to carry out regular maintenance.

Commercial markets. Here those requiring your services will include:

◆ property management companies
◆ estate agents
◆ residents' associations
◆ local authorities
◆ schools
◆ churches
◆ hotels and guesthouses.

While there is nothing to stop you operating in this market, it is something that I would only recommend you do when you have gained sufficient confidence and experience in running your business for the domestic sector.

Property developers and estate agents are not renowned for their speedy settlement of accounts. Neither are local authorities, many of whom deal with such a large volume of outside contractors that payment can take anything up to 90 days.

In fact anyone you work for in the commercial sector will generally not pay you for at least one month from the date of your invoice. This means that you may not have sufficient resources to support both yourself, and your business, during this time.

You'll also need to devote a certain amount of time every month to:

◆ sending out invoices
◆ chasing late payments
◆ attending meetings with management committees and residents' associations.

Then there are the sharks. There are some businesses, particularly those operating in the property management sector, which have no intention of ever paying you and will offer you a comprehensive list of reasons why they shouldn't. And when you insist, they'll simply refer you to their expensive lawyers whose job it is to save them money.

Compare this to the advantages of working in the domestic sector:

◆ Accounts are paid when you complete the work, not 30, 60 or 90 days from invoicing. This means that cash flows into your business on a daily, weekly and monthly basis.
◆ There are more domestic customers than there are commercial ones.

- The competition is not as fierce.
- You don't need any formal qualifications.
- You don't have to be trading for years to succeed.
- Your reputation is built on the quality of your work.
- Generally speaking homeowners are great to work for.
- You can allow far more time to do the work, as pricing isn't based on volume.
- Far more of your time can be spent earning money, as opposed to having to chase it.
- It's more fun!

The market local to you

The market that you will be working in will depend on a number of factors, for example, where you live (be it in a town, city or in the countryside) and the age range of your potential clients.

Another influence is the sort of weather your area gets. It's not uncommon for the South East to be enjoying mild weather while the North and Scotland struggle with freezing conditions. All of these factors will determine your market place. What is important is that you don't see any market factor as being limiting, rather see opportunity in everything. While it's unlikely that you'll be asked to cut lawns in the depth of winter when the ground is frozen, there are lots of other useful services that you can offer your clients during these times. These include:

- repair and maintenance service
- winter digging regime, preparing the ground for spring planting
- frost protection service
- tree and hedge planting
- garden clearance
- re-designing areas for the approaching season.

Your skills and aptitudes

Carry out a skills analysis

Before you start looking at your own individual markets, and working further on market research, you'll need to carry out an analysis of the skills you currently have.

The tools of our business are not too important at this time. Whether or not you have the latest gardening gismo means nothing if you're not able to use it properly.

You will need to identify your own skills and recognise what services you can *immediately* offer. I stress immediately, as knowledge and skills are things which you can acquire and build on as your business grows.

> **Limited skills should not hold you back.**

Make a list

It's time to take a look at yourself in terms of what you can offer potential clients. Remember, if you can cut a lawn then you've enough skill to start your own business. All of the other skills can be acquired and learnt. So don't be put off if you only get one item down on the list.

♦ Begin by listing all the jobs you can think of that will need doing around the garden at any time of the year.

♦ You may find it easier to do this if you divide your list into the 12 months of the year.

♦ Don't limit your list to outdoors. If you're a wizard with houseplants then that is another angle for your business.

♦ Brainstorm your ideas. Do this by writing down everything that comes into your head, no matter how stupid or incredible it may sound.

♦ When your list is completed take a short break before listing all the gardening skills you have.

♦ Remember, everything that you can do in a garden is a skill. The apparently simple act of collecting and bagging autumn leaves is a skill, and something that people will pay you to do.

♦ Skills can be anything from repairing, painting or erecting a fence to sweeping the garden paths. Put everything down.

Interpreting the results

Let's assume that initially at least you've only put down lawn cutting. That's fine, because this is a service in itself. Lawn cutting isn't about fashion, it's about need. Every garden that has a lawn will need it cut either once or twice a week. Thus representing a market for your services. *The most important thing is not to dwell on the fact that all you can do is cut a lawn, but to make sure that you cut lawns better than anyone else.* Aim for the top end of the domestic market where clients will pay extra for a professional cut. Imagine for a moment that your lawn cutting service were a hairdresser's or barber's shop. Are you a £5 short back and sides operation hoping to boost your earnings with tips? Or are you looking to offer the best lawn cutting service in your locality and therefore able to charge more?

> **Whatever you do, make sure you do it well.**

Say your list goes beyond this. Perhaps you're confident at planting and at pruning, or you're an expert on roses or vegetable growing. Maybe you're one of the ever-increasing groups of gardeners who are using organic methods of gardening and are determined to make your garden as environmentally welcoming as possible. Then initially, at least, you're ready to offer a whole range of services that come under the heading of organic:

- organic pest control methods
- preparing the soil using only recognised and approved organic products
- running an organic gardening advisory service.

As I've said before, skills are something that can be acquired and learnt. When it comes to gardening, I don't think anyone would be foolish enough to claim that they know it all. Even the most seasoned of gardeners, who've spent a lifetime caring for and tending gardens, tell me that they learn something new every day. So don't be afraid of what you don't know. Instead, concentrate on what you do know and the rest you can learn as time goes on.

Further research

Libraries are full of gardening books. Huge, wonderful, glossy books full of information and practical advice that are available to you free of charge. At any one time I will have anywhere between three and ten gardening books on loan from the library. Some I take out regularly. Some I need just once for a specific project or job. I have also built up my own comprehensive gardening library. Those books that I have borrowed from the library and found myself going back to again and again, I have eventually bought. To me books are as important as tools. In fact they are such an integral part of your business that buying them is a legitimate business expense and therefore tax deductible.

Have you got what it takes?

In running your own business you will have to:

- rely on yourself
- motivate yourself
- take responsibility for your future
- be flexible
- be your own best friend
- be physically fit
- be mentally prepared.

Below is a list of questions that you should ask yourself. It's useful if you can write down your answers, but don't worry if you can't.

1. Why do you want to work for yourself?
2. What is your biggest fear about starting your own business?
3. Do you enjoy your own company?
4. Can you take criticism?
5. How physically fit are you?
6. What impact will this successful venture have on your current lifestyle? Be specific. For example you may be planning to earn enough money to pay off a large debt, or break free from your present employment.

The objective of the exercise is to help you recognise where in the world of gardening freelance opportunities are most likely to be. Let's have a look at what this has brought out.

Interpreting your answers

1. Why do you want to be self-employed? Certainly being self-employed has its attractions. It's estimated that around 80% of the working population would like to be self-employed. The question is why? Why would so many wish to give up all the rights of an employee to branch out on their own?

While there are lots of advantages to being self-employed, there are also some perks that initially you may have to forego:

♦ regular wage/salary

♦ paid holidays

♦ paid sick leave

♦ the daily social contact with your work colleagues

♦ support in making decisions.

Starting a business from nothing is probably one of the most exciting things that you could ever do, particularly when your business grows and become profitable. But be warned, getting there takes lots of hard work and commitment. You must remember also that you, and you alone are responsible for all that happens in your business. This means sharing in any losses as well as profits.

2. What's your biggest fear? What's stopping you from running your own gardening business? If it's lack of knowledge of the nuts and bolts of setting up and running the business, then you won't have to look further than this book. However, I suspect that lurking somewhere in your mind are other fears. These may include meeting people for the first time, or stepping into the unknown, or worrying that you don't know enough about gardening to do it professionally. My biggest fear was that I didn't know enough about gardening to be able to actually charge someone for my work. If this is yours, don't worry. There are ways that you can increase your knowledge and which will help give you the confidence to get started. Here are some examples:

♦ Evening classes.
♦ Correspondence courses.
♦ Short courses.

- Take a part-time job with a local nursery.
- Read as many gardening books as you can.
- Befriend a local nurseryman or woman. In my experience, nothing quite compares with the knowledge and enthusiasm for plants and plant care than that of these men and women who spend their lives growing things for our benefit. You'll find they'll be only too happy to share their experience with you.

Whatever your greatest fear is, you can overcome it. Decide now to start doing just that.

3. Do you enjoy your own company? Gardening for a living can be a solitary affair. I have worked on a number of projects where apart from an occasional robin following my progress, I have been on my own for the day. This wouldn't suit everyone. I recently took over the management of a large estate where the previous gardener had to resign on the advice from his doctor as he was suffering from depression. His doctor told him that he wasn't suited to working on his own and needed an environment where he was in contact with other people.

4. Can you take criticism? Hopefully the times that your work will be criticised will be few, but there will be occasions where despite your best efforts you will fail to please someone. How will you cope if this happens?

Flying into a defensive rage with your customer will solve nothing. So if you're the type of person who shoots first and asks questions later, you may be better suited to the life of an employee.

Criticism can be constructive, part of the learning experience.

5. How physically fit are you? If you're to be successful and enjoy running your business, being physically fit is a must. There's an enormous difference between clipping and mowing your own lawn for a couple of hours on a Saturday afternoon and spending eight hours a day, five days a week gardening.

Get fit before you start your business.

6. What impact will running a successful venture have on your lifestyle? Can you visualise the impact your successful venture will have on your lifestyle? It's important that you can. Working for yourself, being your own boss, whether it be a few hours a week or every day, means that you alone are responsible for motivating yourself. Particularly in the early days when everything is somewhat unsure, and you've stepped out of your comfort zones, you may find your motivation wavering. This is perfectly normal. When you're on your knees pulling stubborn weeds with a freezing wind biting at your neck, it can be difficult to visualise your success, particularly if you've enjoyed the warmth of working in a comfortable office with fresh coffee on the go and time to phone your friends. Not to mention a regular salary.

Never lose sight of your dream

No matter who you are there will be times that you will lose sight of your dream. The vision of where you want to go will be lost to a deep, seemingly impenetrable cloud of pessimism. You are what you think. If you think you're successful, then in your eyes, you are. If you think you're a failure, likewise, in your mind you are. That's why it's so important that you continually remember why it is you're doing what you're doing.

You must see yourself as being successful right from the start. You're the one with the guts and enthusiasm to start your own business. The muck, sweat and all the rest that goes with it, is part and parcel of your new life. From now on you're going to be paddling your own canoe, often not really knowing what's around the next turn. Being responsible for your own future brings with it a number of challenges and one of them is to keep motivating yourself to keep going, especially when times get tough.

> **From now on promise yourself that when you feel de-motivated you'll turn to your vision of the successful you as inspiration. Nothing beats the feeling of paddling your own canoe when all around are standing on the bank waiting for ferries that are never going to come.**

How much time will your business need?

Part-time

Running your own gardening business is all about satisfying needs:

- your own needs
- the needs of your customers.

One of the main advantages of running a gardening business is that you are not tied to set opening hours as would be the case were you to have opened a shop. This means you can run your business to fit in around your present commitments. Maybe you only want to work one or two days a week. If so, then the way you run your business will differ from those who wish to make this a full-time, all-year-round business.

Case study

Two years ago, Andy was made redundant. At the age of 48 he wasn't holding out enormous hope of getting another job like his previous one. Wrongly or rightly, he believed that his age would stand against him. Fortunately, at the time of Andy's redundancy, his wife Sally was promoted and received a large salary increase, which meant that financially they had enough to cover their monthly outgoings.

Prior to Andy's redundancy, their two small children were looked after by a nanny while both of them were at work. This was no longer necessary and Andy really enjoyed spending more time with his children. However, he wanted some sort of part-time job to get him out of the house when the kids were at school.

Everyone knew Andy was a keen gardener. His ex-colleagues, with whom he still kept in contact, joked that his garden must be looking fabulous now he was at home all the time. It was. But that was the problem. There was only so much gardening he could do at home. And when one of his friends rang him up and asked him if he'd mind helping them with theirs, Andy jumped at the chance and his part-time gardening business was started.

Andy doesn't advertise his services. There is no need to. He has a small clientele mainly made up of his ex-colleagues and their friends. He doesn't keep regular hours. His only commitment to his business is that he visits his client's garden once a fortnight, at a time convenient to him.

It's an ideal arrangement.

Andy's story is not unique. There are lots of people like Andy who run small, part-time gardening businesses to satisfy their own needs both in terms of income and lifestyle. But what suits Andy may not suit you. Therefore it's important that you work in the area that suits your aspirations and lifestyle.

Full-time

If you're planning to start a full-time business, or at least one that will not involve you relying on already established contacts, such as ex-colleagues or friends, then you will need a more structured approach than in Andy's case.

Chapter 2 looks at business planning and how best you can plan for success.

Finding your niche

Everyone's business will differ in that not everyone will offer the same services. Take a look at any of the advertisements in your local papers or *Yellow Pages* and you'll see what I mean. The term gardening has a very broad meaning.

If you're still stuck for ideas on what types of things you can offer, the list below may help.

Type of services

lawn cutting
weeding
digging
rose pruning
general pruning
specialist pruning
leaf clearance
autumn tidy-ups
spring tidy-ups
greenhouse cleaning
greenhouse repairs
greenhouse erection and building service
frost, bad weather protection for shrubs
    and plants
pest control
organic pest control
driveway, pathway cleaning and weeding
turf laying
specialist water feature building and maintenance

scarifying
aeration
applying lawn enhancement treatments
fence repairs
fence painting
fence erection
transplanting service
tool sharpening service
while on holiday, watering/looking after
    garden service
garden planning
garden design
indoor gardening
gardening coaching
organic gardening service
pot cleaning and recycling
organising garden tours
pond maintenance

Start slowly and build up

The most important thing at this stage is that you don't try to offer something with which you're not familiar. Experience and expertise are things you can work on. But for now at least, there's nothing to be gained by tackling work that you're unsure of, or worse unable to do. Potential clients will think more of you if you tell them upfront that you can't do something, rather than plough ahead and destroy prized shrubs. Even the apparently simple motion of cutting lawns can and is very often done badly. So, initially, try to tailor your service to undertaking tasks that you feel comfortable and confident doing.

My business

I now offer a wide range of services, which include hard landscaping. I say now because I didn't start out with such an ambitious list. I began by offering what I described as 'a professional gardening service'. I was fairly confident in my all-round gardening ability, so I felt comfortable doing this. But what I couldn't do was build walls, lay patios, erect and repair fences. Ironically, one of the first calls was someone asking me to build them a patio! I gracefully declined. Now such an undertaking would be no problem. So don't be put off by not being able to offer as much as you'd like.

> **By starting slowly and building your business you'll find it much more fun and far less frustrating. New skills can be acquired, but all in good time.**

If you've already got qualifications

If you have any special gardening skills or qualifications then obviously the service you offer will be far more specialised than that of the general freelance gardener. Nevertheless don't limit your freelancing to just one service. Being a qualified garden designer is a business in itself, but remember that many clients want an all-in service. So think about either subcontracting building of the garden to a landscaping company, or even doing the work yourself.

Gardening coaching

Whatever your expertise, use it. Being a freelance gardener doesn't mean that you have to spend all your time buried in muck and sweat. Running evening, day or weekend classes in your special subject is well worth considering, particularly during those long winter months. Gardening coaching is another way of using your expertise. You can coach by running courses in either your own or the client's garden. Coaching can be tailored to your client's needs and can be on any subject from propagation to caring for bonsai trees. Coaching isn't for everyone, but if you've got the expertise, knowledge and confidence in your own delivery, this is an excellent way to earn a good income.

Carrying out some initial market research

The importance of research

Every business with something to sell carries out some research before finalising and pricing their product or service. In your case you will need to:

* find out who your customers are likely to be
* identify your competitors
* find out what they are charging
* decide on what services you will offer initially.

Where to find the information

Your local newspaper, council offices, library, free property pages, newsagents' windows, supermarket classified boards are full of information about who your potential clients are likely to be. Try:

* local newspapers
* council offices
* libraries
* free newspapers
* newsagents' windows.

Local newspapers

The classified section will have a number of gardening contractors advertising their services. Study these ads. Try imagining that you are looking to employ a gardener, which one would you choose? Or, if you wouldn't choose any of them, ask yourself why. Don't be put off if there is what appears to be a very large number of companies advertising. There's always room for another professional. Remember, there is only so much that one contractor can do at any given time regardless of how large they may be.

Generally speaking, larger contractors will not look at the smaller jobs. With expensive overheads, they cannot afford to cut Mr and Mrs Johnson's hedge in the morning and spend the afternoon cleaning out someone else's pond. This is where the freelancer wins. You can be flexible enough to cater for any job, no matter how small, while still making a profit. Never underestimate the value of being small. *When it comes to gardening, people love nothing better than a personal service.* Glossy brochures, expensive one-page advertisements in Yellow Pages are nothing compared to what you can offer. So don't let the larger boys dampen your enthusiasm. They're operating in a different market.

Council offices and libraries

By visiting your local council's offices you can learn more about who is living in your locality.

Ask for copies of any reports that illustrate the makeup of the local population. Are you living in an area where the population is predominantly retired? What new housing estates are being planned? What developments are currently underway? Take as much published information as possible away with you. Even if you don't use it now, information like this is invaluable for future business planning.

Free newspapers

Every week *The Property Weekly* falls through our letterbox. It's full of potential clients for our business. As everyone who has moved house knows, the last thing on your list is to sort out the garden. Although it may be in a terribly overgrown state, there are usually umpteen other things that need your attention. Apart from hacking away the brambles to see the front door, initially at least there is little time for the garden. This presents enormous opportunity. You need to be proactive. Don't rely on customers finding you. Instead go looking for them. Scan the property pages and highlight houses with large gardens and those with gardens that are obviously in need of repair. Cut them out and keep them.

Keep an eye out for these properties as you travel about your locality. As soon as you see the sold sign appear, drop a card or letter introducing your services through the letterbox. Or better still wait until the new occupants have moved in and then put your literature through their door. This really is a great way of getting bigger jobs without having to advertise. I've done this with great success. The only problem I found with it was finding enough time to continue doing the initial research. Keep those property pages; they're full of potential properties that could use your services.

Newsagents' windows

Cards in newsagents' windows are a great way to find out who your competitors are and to find potential clients. Browsing your local newsagents' windows and magazine shelves can tell you a lot about who lives in your community and what interests they have. Fellow gardeners advertising their services will also tell you much about going rates for gardening work.

It doesn't have to take hours

Researching your market needn't be something that's hugely time consuming. You don't have to carry out surveys or interview anyone. Your local council have already done it for you. Whichever way you decide to tackle your research, make sure you devote some quality time to it. Your aim is to find out who your customers are likely to be; who your competitors are and what price they're charging. Your local newsagents' magazine racks can give a good indication as to how affluent your area is. Are you living in a *Homes and Garden* neighbourhood, or *Crime Weekly*?

> You can never start your research too soon.

Summary

1. Not only is gardening big business, but there is a desperate shortage of professional gardeners to satisfy what is an ever-growing need. This means that you will find a market for your services without having to rely on price-cutting and price wars to find your first clients.

2. Your business can be as flexible as you want it to be, particularly if you're going to start a part-time venture. But a full-time business will need full-time commitment.

3. Gardening can be physically hard work and it may involve you working long hours on your own. Make sure you've got the right temperament for this before you start.

4. You'll need to carry out some market research to determine who are your customers and who is the competition. Don't worry if there appears to be endless businesses offering gardening services. There will always be room for a professional company.

Essential Planning for You and Your Business

The importance of business planning

Why do so many new businesses fail?

It's estimated that 92% of all new businesses that fail do so as a result of:

- either inadequate or no business planning
- lack of sufficient working capital.

It is therefore essential that you devote sufficient time and energy to your business planning, prior to starting. This means writing a **business plan**.

Planning is something we do already

Whether it's just picking up a newspaper to check what programmes are on television, or phoning to book a table at a restaurant, planning is something we do already. There's nothing magical about it. It's part and parcel of our daily lives. So don't let the idea of having to prepare a business plan turn you off. It really is simple.

> Before I started my business, I bought a book on writing a business plan. It was a lengthy, tedious affair and something that I finally abandoned when the author began to discuss ways of attracting foreign investment to finance new ventures. Somehow, I couldn't quite imagine having to do this to purchase my fork or spade! Clearly the book was written for those looking to borrow vast amounts of money to set up their businesses.

This doesn't mean that planning isn't just as important for running a gardening business as running a major corporation. **In fact, it's more important that we get our figures right as we will not have anything near the resources available to big businesses.**

Your business plan will need to cover:

- Detailing your business idea.
- What costs are involved in starting it.
- How you're going to finance your business.
- Preparing a forecast of your anticipated sales.
- Preparing a forecast of your anticipated expenditure.
- Looking at how much you're likely to earn.
- Finally, deciding if your original idea is viable. If it is, then fine. If not, don't worry. Far better to find that your idea isn't as profitable as you thought it was, as opposed to starting with something that is doomed from the word go.

Business planning is what secures your business' future.

Case study

John the builder

I met John while taking a break from a heavy gardening job. We were both having coffee and a roll in a local café. Seeing my van outside, he asked if I was a builder. When I told him I was a self-employed gardener, he scoffed and said that he'd tried running his own business and given up.

Here's what he told me. John had decided it was time to start his own business when he had become tired and disillusioned working for others; the middlemen, as he called them. Builders who charged a great deal for the hard work that he did, while paying him a much-reduced rate.

He was a qualified, experienced painter and decorator who could also turn his hand to any other type of building work. He was an easygoing, likeable person who enjoyed chatting to people while he painted their houses. So when he began telling them that he was thinking of starting his own decorating firm, promises of work flowed in.

To put it in his own words: 'I decided to stop talking about it and just do it. Like what it says on the T-shirt.'

He left his employment on Friday evening and opened for business the following Monday morning. Prior to starting he had already secured his first client, an amiable lady who wanted the downstairs part of her house painted.

Full of enthusiasm, John painted his first client's house. She was delighted with the results. His workmanship was flawless. He cleaned up every evening after he'd finished. He was a pleasure to have in the house. She trusted him enough to be able to leave him alone while she went out. When she told this to her neighbours, they all wanted him to come and paint for them.

Everything was going well. John's wife was delighted. Initially, she had been very worried when he'd told her that he was leaving his job to start out on his own. With a family of small children to feed and a substantial mortgage to pay, she'd naturally thought he was better off working for someone else. After all, he'd enough responsibilities without looking for more. But when John was working every day of the week, she was naturally relieved, and eventually came round to the idea of him being self-employed.

But there was a problem. One that neither of them had foreseen: John was rushed off his feet, but he wasn't earning any money. While there was an ever-growing list of clients waiting for John's services, none of these jobs were actually profitable.

The problem stemmed from John's first client. When he'd quoted for her job, he hadn't really given much thought to how much he was going to have to spend on materials and all the other things like tools and ladders. These weren't important to him then. He felt it was more a priority to find his first client, impress her with the quality of his workmanship and then look at his prices.

This resulted in the job being priced too low. Word spread quickly, and unwittingly John had become the cheap and cheerful of the decorating trade.

He was now earning less than he was when he'd been employed and he was having to work longer hours. The harder he worked, the more acute became his problems. Bills mounted. Then there were the things he'd never budgeted for, expenses such as Public Liability Insurance.

He managed to survive eight months by propping up his business with his savings, and when those were exhausted, he borrowed money using his credit card.

In a final, desperate attempt to salvage his business, he raised his prices on work he'd already agreed to do. The result was devastating. Customers cancelled orders. Rather than seeing him as the conscientious, hard-working individual that he was, people perceived him as greedy. Everyone could see how busy he was, and they all assumed that if he was busy he was doing well. Even his wife was fooled. It was only when he'd finally ran out of available credit that he was forced to close his business.

Learning from others' mistakes

John's experience is not unique. Many people who start a business do so with plenty of enthusiasm and a real desire to succeed. However, *this is not enough*. There are some valuable lessons to be learnt from John's case study:

◆ It vital that you discuss your idea with those closest to you, particularly those who share your life. Arriving home one day and announcing to your husband, wife or partner that you have given up the day job, and decided to garden full-time for a living, isn't the way to do it. Discuss your plans fully with those who share your life. If your business is to succeed then it's vital that it has everyone's support and not just yours.

◆ You must prepare a viable, achievable business plan, one that considers all aspects of your idea.

◆ When it comes to pricing your service, undercutting and offering your work at rates that are far lower than the market expects will only lead to trouble.

◆ Your idea must be profitable. If your sole aim is for your business to pay you a wage, then it's probably better to find a job working for someone else. You'll certainly find it easier and you'll enjoy perks such as paid holidays.

◆ You must forecast your expenditure as well as your sales. Failure to do this will mean that you will be unable to work out whether or not your business is viable.

Planning a strategy

Plan for success, not failure

By setting up your own gardening business you will be taking yourself on one of the most life-changing journeys imaginable. Give yourself the best possible future by deciding to plan for success, not failure. Take the time to carry out your initial research in terms of:

◆ Who are your customers?
◆ Who is your competition?
◆ What are the going rates?
◆ How much is providing your service going to cost?
◆ What will make customers want to use you as opposed to your competitors?

Don't be put off by doom and gloom statistics. Business experts seem to like nothing better than reminding would-be entrepreneurs, people like you, that two out of every three new businesses fail within six months, and of those that survive, only a small percentage last beyond three years. This need not be you.

Two vital strategies

- First **plan to survive**.
- Then **plan to succeed**.

Survival planning

Being able to get by and live through those initial and often difficult days or months is a task in itself. So accept that there are challenges ahead. Be prepared for some hard work. Certainly in the early days, when you're striving to establish your business, things don't always look too rosy. But don't be put off by this.

   Imagine your business is a young plant, or a seedling. Before it can grow into a healthy, mature plant it will have to overcome some fairly tough obstacles. Anything from trying to break through ground as hard as concrete to coping with the elements. Eventually, however, most break free and grow into something truly magnificent, just as your business will.

> Survival and success go hand in hand. If you don't learn how to survive,
> you cannot possibly succeed.

Planning for success

Success is where you achieve your dreams and ambitions. These could be:

- To earn enough money to pay off a debt.

- To pay for the children's school fees, a holiday, or home improvements.

- A life changing experience, where you break free from whatever hell you're in now and become truly independent running your own business.

When I started my first goal was to be able to earn enough money to pay my bills. But my vision for success went far beyond this. My criteria for success were relatively simple. I wanted to:

◆ have a successful, profitable business
◆ have fun
◆ enjoy each day as opposed to dreading the next
◆ create beautiful gardens that inspire.

Success to me in those first crucial months was not about earning huge sums of money or taking lots of time off, but surviving, managing to earn enough money to pay my bills.

While surviving can be considered success in itself, I believe that it is dangerous to rely solely on earning just enough to pay your way. You will need to want more.

Earning little or no money and working long hours can lead to resentment and before you know it you'll end up like poor John. So, make it your goal to *survive first and then succeed thereafter*. Believe me, it's a lot less frustrating, far more achievable than living in cloud cuckoo land and hoping your new business will deliver all your dreams in its first month or year.

What does success mean to you?

Before moving on to writing your business plan, write a few lines on what success will mean to you. Then when you're happy with what you've written put it somewhere you can see it every day. You'll be surprised how quickly you will achieve your ambitions.

> **Seeing yourself as successful is the first step towards achieving success.**

Writing Your Business Plan

This is your plan

Even if you're undecided as to what your business or operation is going to be like, you'll find the following exercise of writing even a rough idea of how your future business is going to operate is worthwhile. You may find it easier to read through this section in its entirety before writing your plan. By the end of the exercise you will have a greater appreciation of what your business will be like and how much money you're going to need to set it up.

Whatever way you want to tackle this, remember this is your plan. You don't have to show it to anyone at this stage. A business plan is not a legal requirement for any business. You will only have to show this to anyone if you wish to borrow money to start your enterprise. Writing a plan before you start will show you what you need to do in order to achieve your goals. If the plan doesn't deliver, then all you have to do is re-write it. I wrote countless plans before I started, so be ready for more than one attempt.

Guidelines for writing your business plan

- Always be realistic in your planning.
- Accept that you may have to write a number of plans before you're finally satisfied that your plan is complete.
- A good idea is to write three separate plans
  - the first, detailing your worst-case scenario
  - the second, what you think is achievable and finally
  - the third, your ultimate plan.
  This is the one that you'd really like to achieve but have some, if not many, reservations about.
- Whatever your plan, make sure it includes a contingency plan.

Describe your current financial health

This is one of the most awful things that I had to do - describe on paper my financial health. Depending on your personal circumstances, past and present spending habits, this can be a fairly stressful exercise, but worthwhile and essential.

You will need to:

- Detail all your present outgoings.
- Deduct any regular incomes, for example part-time salary, pension, etc.

The difference between what you spend and what income you currently have is known as **survival income**. The minimum amount of money you will need to earn every month in order to say afloat.

Don't confuse survival income with what you will ultimately want to pay yourself.

Survival income planner

What I need to pay every month

Mortgage/rent	£
Loan re-payments (total all)	£
Credit card repayments	£
Home and contents insurance	£
Gas/electricity	£
Telephone	£
Mobile phone	£
Food	£
Council tax	£
Car, including insurance	£
Car tax (divide annual fee by 12)	£
Other expenses	£
Total expenditure	**£**
Survival income	**£ (equals total expenditure)**

Shocked? Don't worry; this had me breaking out in a cold sweat too. For those of you who are enjoying excellent financial health and your current income exceeds your expenditure, congratulations! Working out your survival income is the first part of assessing your financial health.

How long could you survive without earning, or achieving your survival income?

With prudent planning and careful research, this is a situation you shouldn't arrive at. However, it's possible and even likely that in the early days your business will not earn enough to cover your survival income. I stress that this is in the early days. To carry you through this period we need some cash reserve. This is known as *working capital*.

Survival income is too high: if your survival income is on the high side and you have no working capital, then don't despair. You can still start your gardening business. How about beginning on a part-time basis with your objective being to reduce your personal debt, or building up a cash reserve so that you have enough to get by in that initial period when you go full-time?

Be honest: make sure that you're honest with yourself. You're planning for success – you don't want your business to be another statistic. So really look at your spending. If at present you're earning a large salary, which is unable to meet and cover your monthly outgoings, it is most unlikely (not impossible) that your business will initially be in a position to redress the balance.

Consider a part-time business

If you're earning a relatively good salary at the moment and are unable to meet your current financial commitments, i.e. you've always too much month left over and not enough money, then I would advise you to think very carefully about starting a full-time operation. Your business needs room and breathing space to grow. *Turn a negative into a positive and start part-time.* Start working to pay off whatever debts are keeping you stuck where you are. You'll have great fun doing it. Before long you'll be ready to leap full-time into your business.

> **Survival income is the most important income of all.**

Detailing your business idea

In Chapter 1 we had a look at what skills you have. Now it's time to put that together with your business idea and write a short paragraph, which describes your business. Ten or so lines should be sufficient. If you've already thought up a name for your business, great, use it. When describing your business and the services you're going to offer try to:

- be specific
- be creative
- be adventurous
- be positive.

Your business statement

'My gardening service is initially going to be run part-time so that I can fit it around my present commitments. I can start by offering the following services...'

You're not writing an ad so don't worry if it sounds terrible. You're not going to be showing this rough draft to anyone.

Describing your service

Do you want to build a gardening round where you have regular clientele with weekly or fortnightly appointments? A lawn cutting service that includes sweeping paths and cleaning borders as you go? Or are you only going to undertake the larger jobs where you quote in advance for your work and do not charge hourly rates?

The business you choose to start will depend on a number of factors:

◆ your own personal requirements
◆ the market place peculiar to where you live
◆ what's already being offered in your area.

Review your plan regularly.

Don't be surprised if, by the end of the book, your original plan differs from what you put down now.

> I review my business plan on a quarterly basis and I'm constantly looking to improve upon what I'm offering my customers and streamlining my business.

The most important thing to remember about your plan is that it must be both flexible and adaptable. Throughout this book we'll be looking at ways of ensuring your enterprise stands a good chance of passing through survival and entering the successful stage. To do so, both you and your plan must be open to change.

What costs are involved in starting your business?

Now that you have decided on a rough outline of what services you are going to offer, you will have a greater idea of what you need to have in order to provide these services.

The tools of your trade

> When I first started out I used the tools that I already had. Generally, this was fine. However,

I decided that my small electric lawn mower was neither suitable nor capable of cutting some of the lawns I was being asked to do. Many of my new clients were out at work when I visited which meant that there was no way of plugging in my mower. Clearly my electric mower was unsuitable for these jobs yet ideal for gardens that had no side or rear access (you'd be surprised how many exist), which meant having to carry my mower through the main hallway and out of the back door. Thus I had to buy a new mower.

There's no need for you to buy anything. If you're planning to operate a small gardening round, where you visit your clients on a regular basis, weekly or fortnightly, it's possible that you won't have to buy your own tools. Instead you can use theirs. In my experience this can be most satisfactory and means that you can travel to and from your jobs either on foot or on a bicycle, which really does reduce your operating costs.

The only real drawback with using your clients' tools is that to begin with they may need sharpening and some tender loving care. But this is merely an initial inconvenience.

Larger operations

If you're planning a larger operation you will need to give some thought to acquiring your own tools.

Buy the best.

Strong, quality professional tools are worth their weight in gold. Don't be tempted to rush out and buy cheap, DIY store branded goods. Believe me, they're not designed for the sort of punishment you're about to inflict on them. *Buy the very best you can afford.* I've lost count of the amount of cheap tools that I bought in my early days that lasted less than a week and had to be flung in the bin. It's a false economy and a costly mistake that you should avoid.

Guidelines for buying tools

◆ Buy the very best that you can afford.

◆ If you can't afford to do that, don't buy at all.

◆ Electric tools are generally cheaper to buy than their petrol counterparts, but don't be tempted to buy them for this reason. Petrol tools mean you can work anywhere with your own independent tool supply and are safer in damp weather.

◆ Buying used equipment is fine, but make sure that what you buy is of sufficient quality to do the job.

◆ Remember, whatever you buy will most probably be used every day. You're no longer a once a week gardener. Your tools will need to be able to work as hard as you do.

◆ Always buy from a reputable source and get a receipt.

We'll take a more detailed look at tools, what to buy and where to get them in Chapter 3.

When calculating your initial start-up costs only include those items you need now and try to avoid buying everything in one go.

Start-up costs planner

Tools	£
Stationery	£
Advertising	£
Telephone	£
Protective clothing	£
Training	£
Insurance	£
Other expenses	£
Estimated total start-up costs	**£**

If you're unsure what figure you should include, then give an estimate. We'll look at what insurance you may need in Chapter 3. Costs of insurance vary a great deal depending on who you are, what you've claimed for in the past, where you live and so on. For planning purposes budget on at least £200 to cover third party liability.

Using your home telephone or having a dedicated business line

Whether or not you use your own personal telephone for business use is your decision. I installed a separate business line when I first began so that I was able to know for sure if the caller was a client or not. I felt the investment was worth it for the professional image alone. Depending on your budget, you may wish to postpone this until your business starts earning cash. But remember if you do this, then a proportion of your early clients will be calling you on your home phone.

A separate business line has many advantages:

◆ You don't have to change your number some months down the line.

◆ You can deduct the charges, including installation, as tax expenses. All things considered, I feel the investment in my business line was worth it.

◆ If you use the family line, then potential clients can only get through to you when the line is free. If your phone is forever unavailable then all your hard work amounts to nothing.

Financing your new venture

While it is unlikely that your new venture is going to costs thousands to get underway, you will need to have some money available to get started. You'll also need money available to pay your weekly businesses expenses, which may include:

◆ fuel for your lawn mower, car etc
◆ dumping costs
◆ materials
◆ miscellaneous costs.

In the early days you will need to have either cash or credit available to cover these expenses. The smaller the operation you are planning, the less you will have to have available.

In the future, as you expand your range of services and build your business, you may need to get outside help from banks or other lending institutions, but you should be able to cover your initial start-up costs yourself.

My rule for buying new things for my business is that if I haven't got the cash to buy it, I can't afford it. It's kept me from going over budget, something that's very easy to do.

What's in a name?

What you call your business is important.

◆ Be wary of using clichéd names. There are far too many Joe Bloggs, the West Country's answer to Groundforce, or Mary Silver, Green Fingers Gardening Services.

◆ Try to be upbeat and upmarket when deciding on what to call your venture.

◆ Avoid choosing a name that suggests what you're offering is cheap and cheerful.

Be imaginative, inspiring and remember that your name will be with you for as long as you're in business.

> When I carried out my initial market research for my venture, I discovered that people in my area liked doing business with a person as opposed to a business. Potential customers told me that they are far more comfortable phoning a named person, as opposed to a business name. Thus I called my venture Paul Power Landscapes.
>
> I'm confident that my company will deliver what we say we'll do. I'm also proud of achievements in creating and maintaining beautiful gardens. My name is my reputation. My motto is:

You take pleasure, we take pride.

What legal entity are you going to trade as?

Prior to starting, you will need to decide what legal entity your business is going to take. There are a number of options:

◆ limited company
◆ partnership
◆ sole trader.

Limited company

A limited company is a legal entity in its own right. This means that it can sue, or be sued, under its own name. However, the liability of its members is limited to the amount they have invested. A company is not any one individual and is made up of directors and shareholders. It continues to exist in the event of anyone's death. There are lots of regulations on how companies are managed and how they maintain their accounts.

It's unlikely that this will be a suitable entity for your business.

Partnership

The law describes a partnership as 'The relationship which exists between one or more persons carrying on business in common with a view to profit.' A partnership can exist through a verbal or written agreement or by implication.

If you're deciding to start your venture with another person and you both will jointly invest in the business then this a partnership. Although a partnership can exist through a verbal agreement, it makes sense to draw up a written agreement covering all aspects of your planned business, including what will happen if one of the parties wants to leave the business or sell their share. Each partner is equally responsible for all the businesses debts.

If you're considering a partnership, you will have to accept that you will not be the sole decision-maker. *Therefore you have to be very careful with whom you choose to partner*. Many business partnerships consist of husband and wife teams.

Make sure that you have proper written agreements in place. It's worth employing a solicitor to do this for you, for if you fall out with your business partner, or one of you wishes to go a separate way, this may mean having to wind up a successful business.

Sole trader

A sole trader is one who conducts their business by themselves using their own or a business name. This is by far the most common form of legal entity used by most small businesses.

The advantages are:

◆ You, the proprietor, retain full control of your business and its profits and are not bound by the same bureaucracy and regulations as a limited company.

◆ There are no legal requirements for you to have your books externally audited, or have an accountant or for you to register your business name.

Of course you, and you alone, are responsible for everything. It's up to you what entity you trade under, but the vast majority of small businesses of this nature will either trade as a sole trader or partnership. It's unlikely that you will need to form a limited company, at least to begin with. But the decision is yours.

Preparing an initial cash flow forecast

A cash flow forecast demonstrates how you see money coming in and going out of your business on a monthly basis.

Your forecast will include:

♦ your estimated monthly sales figures
♦ less your estimated monthly expenditure.

You need to list all your known regular expenses, such as insurance, telephone, survival income etc and also your estimated expenses.

Why forecast – aren't you just guessing?

No. Forecasting for your financial survival and success is arguably one of the most important aspects of your business plan. You need to have an idea now how much you're going to earn every month and year. I say idea, because at this stage that's all it is. Nobody can predict with any certainty what your earnings are going to be, how fast your business will grow and how quickly you will move from achieving your survival income to realising your success income – profit. But you can set objectives, targets based on what you know, and get a fair idea of what would be a reasonable assumption of what you should be earning. Having now completed some detailed personal and financial analysis you should be in a position to estimate your monthly expenditure.

If you're planning to work at this business part-time, and your earnings will complement an existing income be this a wage from elsewhere or perhaps a pension, don't forget to include this income (net amount) under additional receipts.

> **You should forecast for at least your first year.**

You may wish to plan your first year. Most business plans cover the first three years of trading.

When I first started, I found this impossible. Trying to work out sales in year two when I hadn't yet found my first client in week one was frustrating to say the least.

Try six months initially and then when you feel your plan is realistic forecast the second six months.

Creating a cash flow forecast

The cash flow forecast below (Figure 1) can be copied and adapted to suit your own business needs. The principle will remain the same – *receipts less payments equals net cash flow.*

Monthly cash flow may be either **positive** or **negative**. Obviously your goal is to maintain a healthy, positive cash flow running through your business. However, this will not always be possible. Unforeseen circumstances may have a negative effect on sales, for example bad weather and the like, or something that requires you to take unexpected time off from your business. Therefore it's essential when working out your forecasts that you do not spend all you earn. As I've said before, with this business most expenditure can be foreseen and therefore you should only spend what you've planned to spend. This includes the amount of money you take from the business to pay yourself, which is known as **drawings**.

Receipts

Generally you will only have receipts from cash sales. However, there may be occasions when you receive additional income via other sources, for example if you sell one of your business assets such as a lawnmower. For the purposes of your cash flow you will have:

♦ cash receipts (sales)
♦ other receipts (where you can include anything other than income from sales).

Payments

It's important to create separate columns for all of the common types of expenditure that your business will encounter. Obviously, if you're planning to run a gardening round where you cycle to and from each client you won't need a column for motor vehicle expenses etc. The example below details the following monthly expenditures:

- drawings (what you pay yourself)
- wages and salaries (what you pay everyone else)
- insurance
- postage/printing/stationery
- motor vehicle
- telephone
- dumping fees
- fuel
- other
- stock/materials.

Month	April		May		June		July		August		Sept	
Receipts	Budget	Actual	Budget	Actual	Budget	Actual	Budget	Actual	Budget	Actual	Budget	Actual
Cash sales	700		900		900		1000		500		1000	
Other income												
Total receipts (a)	700		900		900		1000		500		1000	
Payments												
Drawings	500		500		700		700		500		700	
Insurance	63		63		63		63		63		63	
Postage/printing/stationery	5		10		5		10		5		10	
Fuel	40		50		60		60		60		60	
Telephone	65						65					
Dump fees	26		26		55		55		26		26	
Vehicle											35	
Total payments (b)	699		649		883		953		654		894	
Net cashflow (a-b)	1		251		17		47		-154		106	
Opening bank balance	0		1		252		269		316		162	
Closing bank balance	1		252		269		316		162		268	

Fig. 1. RL Gardening Services cash flow forecast.

Notes on expenditure

Insurance

RL Gardening Services have two insurance policies:

♦ vehicle insurance
♦ public liability insurance.

Both policies are paid for in 12-monthly instalments, which equates to a monthly cost to the business of £63. This figure remains constant throughout the cash flow forecast as this cost will only change if the insurance is upgraded in some way to take account of a change in circumstance, for example an additional vehicle or an increase in public liability insurance resulting from taking on additional staff or risk.

Fuel

This is a variable cost and will change from month to month depending on the mileage covered, vehicle being used etc.

Drawings

In this initial cash flow forecast the proprietor of this business has allowed drawings of £500 for the months April and May, £700 for June and July, £500 for August, as this is when he expects to go on holiday and returning to £700 for September.

Telephone

The telephone bill will only be paid twice in this period as this account falls due quarterly. The first payment is made in April, the second in July with the next due in October.

Net cash flow

Cash flow is positive for the first six months of trading with the exception of August where there is a negative cash flow of -£154. If this was my business's cash flow, I would worry about the impact of this and not take holidays until the business has become more established and financially secure.

At the end of the first six months' trading RL Gardening Services forecast shows that the proprietor is expecting to have a cash surplus of £268 in the bank – but this will only be possible if both the financial expenditure and monthly sales targets are achieved.

Comparing forecasts with actual performance

Your initial forecasts are important in that they will give you, the business's proprietor, a great appreciation of what sales you need to achieve to return your desired income. Working out your initial forecasts can be difficult until you fully appreciate the costs particular to your own business. Therefore it's vital that you monitor actual performance against targeted or forecast performance and after the first six months you review all of your initial figures.

RL Gardening Services' completed cash flow analysis for the first six month's trading looks like this.

Month	April		May		June		July		August		Sept	
Receipts	Budget	Actual	Budget	Actual	Budget	Actual	Budget	Actual	Budget	Actual	Budget	Actual
Cash sales	700	900	900	840	900	950	1000	700	500	550	1000	1100
Other income												
Total receipts (a)	700	900	900	840	900	950	1000	700	500	550	1000	1100
Payments												
Drawings	500	500	500	500	700	700	700	700	500	500	700	700
Insurance	63	63	63	63	63	63	63	63	63	63	63	63
Postage/printing/stationery	4	4	10	8	5	10	10	18	5	7	10	9
Fuel	40	65	50	60	60	60	60	50	60	30	60	78
Telephone	65	65		26			65	80				
Dump fees	26	55	26		55		55	26	25	25	26	55
Vehicle							100			35		
Total payments (b)	699	752	649	657	883	933	953	934	654	625	894	905
Net cashflow (a-b)	1	148	251	183	17	17	47	-234	-154	-75	106	195
Opening bank balance	0	0	1	148	262	331	269	348	316	114	162	39
Closing bank balance	1	148	252	331	269	348	316	114	162	39	268	234

Fig. 2. RL Gardening Services cash flow analysis.

Observations on the business's actual performance in relation to its original forecast.

Sales

The business got off to a good start with sales exceeding original forecasts by £200. However, this had a proportionate negative effect on costs and we can see that fuel costs and dumping costs both exceeded original budgets.

In May, month 2, sales failed to reach target as they did in July. The shortfalls, however, have not had a damaging effect on performance as the business retained £224 cash in the bank at the end of its first six months, this being only £44 short of the original forecast.

The unexpected

In June the business' vehicle broke down which resulted in an unexpected repair bill of £100. These are the types of costs that you cannot budget for. However, you must include some provision for maintenance in your forecasts. It would be wise for the business to put aside some money every month, provided of course the business remains in positive cash flow, to cover both unexpected costs and all of the annual costs, for example vehicle MOT, road fund licence, tool replacement etc.

Preparing a profit and loss forecast

While a cash flow forecast will help you predict what monies are likely to flow in and out of your business during any trading period, you may find it useful to prepare a profit and loss forecast.

The difference between a profit and loss forecast and cash flow forecast is that your profit and loss forecast will demonstrate how profitable your business is likely to be based on your anticipated sales and expenditure. It will be particularly useful for any business that sells goods as well as services.

Profit is calculated as follows:

Sales minus your direct costs: costs of materials and wages = gross profit.

Trading profit is worked out by taking your gross profit and deducting all your other business overheads and your drawings (what you pay your self every month).

Net profit is worked out by reducing any depreciation that you may be able to claim. Obviously net profit is the most important figure to concern yourself with as this shows how profitable your business venture is likely to be. The expression 'bottom line' comes from net profit as this is the final figure you arrive at.

Have a look at both the profit and loss forecast and the actual completed profit and loss account for RL Gardening Services.

Month	April		May		June		July		August		Sept	
	Budget	Actual	Budget	Actual	Budget	Actual	Budget	Actual	Budget	Actual	Budget	Actual
Sales (net of VAT)	700		900		900		1000		500		1000	
Less direct costs												
Costs of materials												
Wages												
Gross profit (b)	700		900		900		1000		500		1000	
Gross profit margin (b/a *100%)	100		100		100		100		100		100	
Overheads												
Drawings	500		500		700		700		500		700	
Insurance	63		63		63		63		63		63	
Postage/printing/ stationery	5		10		5		10		5		10	
Fuel	40		50		60		60		60		60	
Telephone	65						65					
Dump fees	26		26		55		55		26		26	
Vehicle											35	
Total overheads (c)	699		649		883		953		654		894	
Trading profit (b-c)	1		251		17		47		-154		106	
Less depreciation												
Net profit before tax	1		251		17		47		-154		106	
Cumulative net profit	1		252		269		316		162		268	

Fig. 3. RL Gardening Services profit and loss.

Month	April		May		June		July		August		Sept	
	Budget	Actual	Budget	Actual	Budget	Actual	Budget	Actual	Budget	Actual	Budget	Actual
Sales (net of VAT)	700	900	900	840	900	950	1000	700	500	550	1000	1100
Less direct costs												
Costs of materials												
Wages												
Gross profit (b)	700	900	900	840	900	950	1000	700	500	550	1000	1100
Gross profit margin (b/a *100%)	100	100	100	100	100	100	100	100	100	100	100	100
Overheads												
Drawings	500	500	500	500	700	700	700	500	500	500	700	700
Insurance	63	63	63	63	63	63	63	63	63	63	63	63
Postage/printing/stationery	5	4	10	8	5	10	10	16	5	7	10	9
Fuel	40	65	50	60	60	60	60	50	60	30	60	78
Telephone	65	65		26			65	80				
Dump fees	26	55	26			55	55	25	26	25	26	55
Vehicle							100			35		
Total overheads (c)	699	752	649	657	883	933	953	934	654	625	894	905
Trading profit (b-c)	1	148	251	183	17	17	47	-234	-154	-75	106	195
Less depreciation												
Net profit before tax	1	148	251	183	251	17	17	-234	-154	-75	106	195
Cumulative net profit	1	148	252	331	252	269	348	114	162	39	268	234

Fig. 4. RL Gardening Services profit and loss.

RL Gardening Services do not have any materials or stock in their books. They simply provide labour. Many gardening businesses will be like this. However, if you're planning to sell plants or provide any materials other than your own labour, you will need to include these costs in your forecasts.

Depreciation

Prior to arriving at your net figure you will see that depreciation is deducted from your trading profit. You are allowed to deduct a certain amount from the value of your assets to cover the asset's wear and tear. This is something that you do not include in your cash flow forecast, and only arrives at the point where you're ready to calculate your net profit.

Calculating depreciation

Allowances that you can claim are set by the government and you check these at the time of preparing your forecasts. Generally you can claim 40% in the first year of your plant and machinery's value and 25% thereafter. Governments also introduce incentive schemes and preferential writing down allowances. For example, from the period 1 April 2000 to 31 March 2003, you can claim 100% for any computers, software or internet technology equipment that you purchase.

Contact your tax office for up-to-date information on depreciation allowances prior to completing any final accounts.

> **Starting a business without forecasts is like jumping into the water without knowing how deep it is – you may or may not survive.**

Contingency planning

Covering the 'what ifs?'

You need to cover yourself in the event that you can't work. There can be a number of factors that can cause this:

- bad weather
- sickness
- accident at work
- family crisis
- personal problems
- other issue.

> **If you anticipate likely problems then you can either plan to avoid them,**
> **or if they happen, plan your escape route.**

While you can't write into your plan guaranteed solutions for overcoming each problem, you must have some form of contingency plan in place. Your business depends on you working, being out there doing what needs to be done. You don't get paid for not working, for the days off you have to take when the weather is too lousy to do anything useful. If you have an accident and can't work then you have no means of earning. Like it or not, gardening is a risky business. You're far more likely to be injured gardening than you are being a victim of crime. Most injuries can be relatively minor, but some may require taking time off to recuperate. *Obviously the best solution is to try to ensure that you stay safe and well and make sure that you adopt safe working practices.*

Business insurance is essential

You should also insure yourself against being unable to work through injury or illness. I have an insurance policy that covers me in the event of my being unable to work due to temporary disablement through an accident at work. It's worth contacting a registered insurance broker and seeing what is available. You'll find those local to you in the *Yellow Pages* or *Thompson Directory*. Pick one that deals with business insurance and ask them to send you some information. There are a lot of insurance products on the market aimed at the self-employed businessperson.

Contingency measures could include:

◆ Having sufficient cash reserves available for a three-month period when you can't work. Longer if you can manage it.

◆ Adequate accident insurance cover that pays a weekly sum in the event that you can't work in your businesses.

◆ Making sure that you adopt safe working practices and continually monitor and look to improve upon your Health and Safety at work.

◆ Reducing the risks you take.

◆ Remembering that you, and you alone, are your service. If you can't perform, then you can't earn.

◆ Looking after yourself.

Case study

As I've told you already, I launched my business because I had to. I did what everybody said not to do and walked out on my job. It was the only way that I could save myself from going insane. I'm not recommending or suggesting that you do the same. If your current job is truly awful and the reason you want to start your gardening is to break free from all the pain, then great. But wait just long enough so you have a clear strategy and a little bit of know-how before telling them where to stick it.

My initial planning

In the months before I left I wrote a number of business plans and gave much thought to how I was going to start my business. My business began with a few humble cards advertising my services in some dreary-looking seaside newsagents. Tucked in between Angie's Mobile Hair Salon, 10% discount for genuine (underlined) OAPS, Greenfingers' Ladies Only Gardening Service and a whole range of other handwritten advertisements offering anything from a clapped out car to a discreet private massage, was my card, advertising Paul Power's Gardening Service. It was a humble beginning. My initial advertising bill was less than £2.50. Having taken £5 with me, I invested the change in a coffee and Danish pastry. I was in business!

Then to my enormous disappointment two weeks had already passed and I hadn't had a single call. It seemed that no one wanted my services. Disappointment turned to disillusionment and all the wonderful images of being self-employed began to ebb away. I was to learn my first hard lesson of running your own business:

You are responsible for own future.

Gone are those weary bosses. Gone too are those colleagues at work you shared your woes with. Now you are entirely responsible for your own destiny. You'll enjoy the wonderful freedoms that being your own boss brings, but you must also find ways through that loneliness that this can bring.

Keeping a positive outlook is vital

I was already feeling low, having just walked out on a regular job, feeling positive was difficult anyway. No, impossible. Which is why I decided to take myself out of the house, where the walls were fast closing in, and off to a nice seaside café, where I sat sipping a coffee and working on a new business plan.

My previous plans had been cautiously optimistic. I hadn't figured on not being able to find any clients at all, which obviously was a bit of a problem. So I spent the morning working on a sales strategy that included running an advertisement in the local paper. The more I worked on my strategy the more positive I became about my future. And by the time I left the café, psychologically I was back on a more positive footing. Even with no clients, no money and lots of bills to pay, I was still happy that I had chosen to start this business.

Why? Because I'd managed to figure out a way through my problems by identifying what was wrong and working on possible solutions. The mere exercise of doing this had changed me from negative to positive. Of course there was no guarantee my new strategy would work, but at least I was working on making my business happen and feeling better for it. Watching the poor waitress flying around the café, rushed off her feet, being barked at by her supervisor, had also made me realise that the dream of self-employment was worth fighting for.

Be prepared to be your own motivator

Whenever you feel down, get out of wherever you are, find somewhere you feel comfortable and take a fresh look at your problems. Don't expect to solve them all. Just work on a few possible solutions. I believe that it's so important to you and your business that you develop a habit of self-reliance. You have ample resources to pull yourself through the difficult times, and believe me there will be some ahead.

When I returned home full of positive energy again, with a new sales strategy all worked out, I nearly didn't see the red light flashing on the answerphone. But when I did, I was overjoyed. Finally, a call from my first prospective client!

'Mr Power, I was wondering if you could help me. I've got a small side garden which is completely overgrown and needs something doing with it. Do you think you could fit me in?'

This lovely lady will never know just how much that telephone call meant to me. Finally (two weeks can seem an eternity when you're waiting for the phone to ring) I had my first client. That morning I had felt dejected and down as I reluctantly pulled myself out of the bed to face another day in my struggling business. That evening, having visited that lady, quoted for what she wanted done, agreed the price and start date, it finally seemed that my business was up and running and for the first night in many weeks I enjoyed an uninterrupted night's sleep. But there was still lots and lots more work to be done on the planning front as I was soon to find out.

Lessons learnt

◆ Learn to develop self-reliance as soon as you can.

◆ Nothing stays the same for long. No matter how terrible things seem, the bad times will pass.

◆ You can only find solutions by first identifying the problem. In my case, I was naive to expect floods of enquiries the moment I advertised my services.

◆ If everything is getting on top of you, take yourself off to somewhere you enjoy and do your thinking there.

◆ No problem is insurmountable.

◆ Being self-employed means just that – you are responsible for employing you!

When the going gets tough

When things go wrong, as they often do for any business, whether small or large, it's easy to become negative and despondent. Unless you are fortunate enough to be surrounded by self-employed business gurus, already enjoying success, there can be little in the way of encouragement. Well-meaning friends, family and all sorts of people will leap to your defence with unhelpful comments like 'don't worry, so and so went out of business and they'd been at it for years'. We end up agreeing with them; it was a silly idea anyway. There you have one reason why two out of every three new businesses fail – because the owners weren't prepared for the enormous changes that running your own business has on your life.

Is your idea viable?

So far in business planning you have looked at:

◆ How much money you need to earn each and every month to keep a roof over your head and the wolf from the door.

◆ Analysing your skills. By now you should have a fairly good idea of some, if not all, of the services you are going to initially offer to prospective clients.

♦ Cash flow and the importance of keeping money flowing through the business so that you can meet private and business commitments.

Are you prepared for self-employemnt?

Prior to starting I'd filled two A4 pads with projections, which ranged from the sensible to the ridiculous. Nothing wrong with that and I strongly urge you to work out as many projections as you possibly can. But what I hadn't done was address the question of my own personal capabilities of running my own business. I'd never really given much thought to what it would be like to run my own show other than the obvious; that I'd be my own boss, no commuting, terrible office politics and having my future career managed and manipulated by people who I could only think of as idiots.

> **But were I to be honest with myself, was I really much better than them at managing my fledgling business?**

Was I really capable of running my own business and making it successful enough so that I didn't have to become an employee again? In hindsight, I don't think I was. Now if my phone didn't ring for a few days, let alone a couple of weeks or longer, I would implement my direct sales strategies. We'll look at what these are later, but for the moment I'll just say that I now wouldn't sit around waiting for business to come to me, I'd be out there actively looking for it.

Phones don't ring unless you do something that makes people want to call you and ask for your help. That makes sense, but here's the difficult part – have you got what it takes to go out there and make your phone ring? Before you answer yes, take the self-profile test based on some of the skills that I either had when I first started, or quickly acquired after I launched my business.

The self-profile test

1. Are you somebody who constantly needs encouragement from friends, family and everyone else?

2. Do you enjoy working on your own?

3. Could you spend all day working in a garden without speaking to anyone, come home exhausted and do it again the following day and the day after?

4. Once you decide to do something do you do it, wait, or leave it until you've changed your mind?

5. Do you have lots of physical and mental energy?

6. Are you in good health?

7. Can you and you alone take responsibility for your own future?

8. Can you take responsibility and deal with difficult situations when whatever has happened wasn't really your fault?

9. Can you deal with a whole variety of people, many of them wonderful and lovely to work with, some of them awful and people you'd normally avoid?

10. Can you learn to live with constant change and a degree of uncertainty and see these as positive, necessary things in your life?

This is not a point scoring exercise and it's certainly not a horoscope, but from your answers you should be able to see what areas you'll have to work at. This is an odd business in that often you'll be working alone in a garden with only the birds and plants for company, while on other occasions you'll be working so close to the homeowner that it'll be like having a relationship with them. The gardeners' world is full of extremes. Then there's the weather, which can be anything from lousy to glorious. Can you learn to enjoy working outside in all weathers?

Summary

1. You must work out your monthly survival income.

2. Plan to survive first and then succeed.

3. Calculate your anticipated start-up costs.

4. Work out how you are going to finance your start-up costs.

5. Decide what legal entity will you will use, be it sole trader, partnership or limited company.

6. Work out an initial cash flow forecast.

7. Work out an initial profit and loss forecast.

8. Discuss your plan with those whose life will be directly affected by it – wife, husband or partner.

9. Give adequate thought to contingency planning.

10. Remember to be realistic in your planning.

Good planning requires solid preparation

You don't have to have it all worked out at this very early stage. What matters is that you start thinking about these things and looking for answers to the questions. *Face the music and calculate what your survival income will need to be – the most important figure at this time.* Knowing how much you need to earn every month to meet your commitments is essential for the future success of your business. Without this information you could well be on the road to financial ruin, which is something to avoid at any costs even if it means you decide you are not financially sound enough at the moment to give up your job and start full-time. Remember, your initial objective in starting this business can be to clear your debt. Then when you're not as over-committed as you are now, you're ready to launch yourself full-time.

There is no reason why your business should fail if you plan for it to succeed.

CHAPTER THREE

What's Involved in Starting and Running a Gardening Round?

Take a look behind the scenes.

Knowing what you're letting yourself in for

The gardening round

> I started my first gardening round when I was 13. With only two customers — the parish priest and an elderly friend of the family — Saturday mornings were spent tending to their gardens.
>
> It was a wonderfully simple business to run. I turned up at a time convenient to myself, mowed the lawns, tended to the flowerbeds and wrestled with the occasional stubborn weed. It was wonderful. Payment was received as soon as I'd finished the work. Marvellous!

Starting a gardening round is one of the easiest things to do. It involves little in the way of capital and can be tailored to fit around your lifestyle, which makes it ideal for anyone wanting to generate an additional part-time income. It's relatively simple to set up, easy to run and the start-up costs are fairly low, if non-existent, but for one necessary expenditure – public liability insurance. There are no high overheads to contend with every month. And if you like security and dislike having to continually sell yourself and your business, then this could be for you.

What's involved?

Setting up your gardening round involves finding enough clients to fill all the available space in your diary, visiting your clients on a weekly, fortnightly or monthly cycle depending on their requirements. *When your diary is full you will no longer have to invest time and money in attracting new clients.*

Sales forecasts

Predicting your earnings is relatively straightforward as you will know how many hours you are going to garden every week and at what hourly rates less your expenses.

For example, if you intend to work 20 hours per week charging £8 per hour, then your gross income will be 20 x 8 = £160. From this you will need to deduct your expenses, but at least your overall income is relatively predictable.

Ideal for part-timers

Gardening rounds are ideal if you want to work part-time, fitting your business around your present commitments. While it's a sure way of earning additional income, it does have certain disadvantages. Your business depends on your continued reliability, i.e. turning up every week, fortnight or month when you say you will. Fail to do this and your reputation will go before you and your round fall to your competitors. Certainty comes at a price. So if you're not going to be able to commit yourselves to regular visits then obviously this business isn't for you.

Seasonal nature

The main drawback with this as a business is that it tends to be seasonal. That of course may suit you. But if like me you want to work full-time in your business, then this may not be the business for you.

The main advantages of running a traditional gardening round are:

◆ Relatively low start-up costs.

◆ Easy to plan and predict your earnings.

◆ You don't have to always use your own tools.

◆ Can be profitable if your prices are set correctly.

◆ There's less selling to do.

◆ You get to know your clients very well.

◆ Ideal for part-timers who want to earn additional income or full-time gardeners who want a regular round without having to constantly advertise and look for new clients.

The main disadvantages are:

◆ What you earn depends entirely on how many hours you garden.

◆ Can be very hard work where clients employ you to do the heavy tasks like weeding and such like.

◆ Earnings can be greatly reduced during periods of bad weather.

◆ Seasonal business – spring to autumn.

◆ Running a round can be more like having a job than managing a business.

◆ Most clients expect you to remove garden debris from site, such as lawn clippings, pruning remains, weeds etc. Costs involved in doing this can be prohibitive.

Working out the costs of providing your service

The costs

While this is a relatively straightforward business to run, your earnings will depend on keeping your costs as low as possible. If you're to succeed it's vital that you get your pricing right.

Too low and you'll end up working for nothing. Too high and you won't get any customers.

Here are the main costs that you are likely to incur when providing this service:

◆ purchasing tools
◆ servicing and repair costs
◆ fuel costs
◆ dumping fees
◆ insurance
◆ your time
◆ tax.

Whether to use your tools or your clients'?

This is very much a matter of personal preference and of course depends on whether or not your clients have in fact got their own tools.

My own experience is that most of my customers have a variety of tools, usually rusting away somewhere in their garage or shed, and have been more than happy for me to use them.

This means that you may not have to rush out and buy your own tools to start this business. Of course you may have most of what you need already to start with.

But for those who either don't have, or won't have access to tools, here's some advice on acquiring tools.

Tools

You'll need a range of gardening tools including: clipping shears, hand pruning tool, shovel, fork, rake, gardening gloves, boots, watering can. In addition you may need a lawnmower depending on whether or not you include lawn cutting. Most garden tools that you buy from the DIY store are great for gardening once or twice a week. Using your tools every day is an entirely different matter, so you will have to include in your costings enough money to replace tools when they break, wear out or worse still get lost. No matter how careful you are there will come a time when you will have to replace even the highest quality tools.

I've lost count of the amount of spades and pruning shears that I've had to replace in the course of my work.

Petrol/diesel

If you're planning to cycle, walk, get the bus or use something other than motorised transport and you don't intend using a petrol lawnmower, then great. You can become one of the growing band of eco-friendly gardeners and won't have to budget for petrol. But if you are using your car and petrol-powered equipment then make sure you include this in your figures. The cost of petrol doesn't look as if it's going to fall dramatically. If anything it will continue to rise. Make sure you include generous allowances to cover fuel and oil.

Servicing and repairs

Your power-driven tools will need to be serviced from time to time and may need to be repaired. These are costs to your business. As a general rule make sure you allow at least £150 per season, per lawnmower, for routine servicing.

Disposing of garden debris

Never underestimate how much even the smallest of gardens produce in the way of unwanted materials. Of course it would be ideal if all our clients had composters and were happy to compost their lawn cuttings, pruning materials etc. However, the reality is that many aren't and they expect their regular gardener to take all unwanted materials off to the dump or wherever, provided it's well away from their gardens. If this is the case then you must include in your costings adequate provision for disposing of waste.

Don't fall foul of the law.

While most local authority amenity tips provide areas for garden waste, they only provide this service for householders. You are no longer a householder, but a professional gardener running a commercial enterprise. They are well within their rights to turn you away at the gate. You may be wondering how they will know that you're running a business. The frequency of your visits and the sheer abundance of materials you are getting rid of will give the game away. You may get past the gate during the first few weeks of trading but sooner or later they'll start hounding you.

Disposing of trade waste at an amenity tip is an offence. By doing so you not only run the risk of being prosecuted and facing heavy fines, but also having your details published in your local paper, which is hardly the sort of publicity that will do your business any good.

Therefore it is essential that you agree in advance with your client an extra charge for removing any debris from site. Alternatively your client may wish to dispose of their own waste.

If your client wants you to take all the waste away, which will generally be the case, you will have to either:

◆ Have a suitable dumping area or skip area set aside in your own property and have it emptied when needed.

◆ Take the debris to a Council Trade Waste Transfer Site, or other such site run by private contractors.

Skip at your own property

If the size of your property will allow it, you could hire a skip on a long-term basis to be emptied once a month. But unless you have planning permission to run a business from home, you will be on very thin ice if your neighbours start complaining about the smell coming from your skip. Let alone having to put up with the aromas yourself.

Waste transfer station for trade refuge

The other option is for you to take it to a commercial site and pay for its disposal. Charges for this vary throughout the country so you'll need to check with your local authority to see how much it's going to cost. There will also be a minimum charge.

> **The commercial tip that I use has a minimum charge of £28 regardless of whether you dispose of one bag or a trailer load. One ton of debris costs £58.**

Make sure you shop around, as there are many private contractors who will allow garden refuge to be dumped on their sites for far less than the local authority ones.

> **Whatever you do, make sure it's cost-effective.**

To make this method cost-effective you need to have a fairly large, high-sided trailer, just like the ones you see the landscaping companies use. You must also remember that you will spend time going to and from the tip then queuing to have your load weighed before you finally manage to dump.

Disposing of rubbish, even garden waste, is one of the most contentious issues at the moment. You can expect hefty fees for being allowed to do so. *Investigate these costs and work out how you're going to get rid of all the waste you accumulate before you finally decide on your hourly rate.*

Insurance

Whatever business you decide to run you will need some form of third party insurance cover to indemnify you from being sued. Accidents can and do happen and whether or not it's your fault doesn't always matter.

Accidents do happen.

Say for example that you visit Mr and Mrs Garden once a fortnight to mow their lawn, weed their borders and do a general tidy-up. You spend four hours doing this and you charge them £40. They're very pleased with your work. You like them. They're a nice friendly couple who always bring you a cup of tea half way through your work and insist on you having a ten-minute break. Everything's going well until one day you're hoeing the back border right next to the conservatory, when Mr Garden comes to ask if you would like another cup of tea, and you stand up suddenly and without thinking swing the hoe round and it shatters the conservatory window. Bang. Mr and Mrs Garden are both extremely upset. They saved hard to pay for the conservatory and a new window is going to costs hundreds of pounds. You too are shocked because you're now thinking how are you going to pay for it? It was you who broke the window and whether or not you could argue that it was Mr Garden's fault for startling you like that doesn't matter. This is the sort of thing that insurance is for. You'll probably have to pay the first £200 of the claim, but let's imagine for a moment that someone is injured in the accident. What do you do then? What happens when dear old Mr and Mrs Garden sue you? The only solution is to have adequate insurance in place to cover you.

You must have adequate Public Liability Insurance in place prior to starting your round.

Your time

How much will you need to earn an hour? By now it should be clear that if you want to earn £8 an hour then you would have to charge more, probably somewhere in the region of £10 an hour.

As a guideline you should add a minimum of 20% to the hourly rate you wish to earn so that you're able to cover the costs of providing the service and still earn what you wanted to. This is purely an estimate. Costs will vary from business to business. So if you're able to walk or cycle to all of your clients, use their tools, lawnmower, and petrol and not have to dispose of any of the debris then the only cost you'll have is your insurance.

Tax

For every weed you pull and every blade you cut, the tax man will want his share of your earnings. What you pay in tax depends on your personal circumstances and tax allowances. It's impossible within the scope of this book to estimate how much tax you're likely to pay, but important to say that you are required by law to keep a record of all your business income and expenditure. These records must be kept for five years following the date of you last tax return. You must also pay a contribution towards your National Health Insurance. This amounts to little more than £2 a week and is paid weekly or monthly.

Can I really earn a decent income running a gardening round?

Yes. Don't be put off by the costs. You may well think that running a gardening round is an expensive business. It can be if you do it properly. However, it can also be profitable, provided you charge enough. This is the key to making this type of business successful.

> **You must get your hourly rates right from the start. Whatever figure you want to earn, as a rule of thumb add no less than 20% to cover your costs. I'd even go as far as 35%.**

This still leaves a lion's share of the income for you. Provided you include enough in your hourly rate to allow for a decent return to yourself, enough to cover costs and a little on top for profit, you can earn a decent income from this type of business. Generally, this is a seasonal business, which runs from spring to autumn. Sadly, when the last of the leaves have been swept away your clients may not require you until the spring when everything starts to grow again.

> **Generally, your prices are fixed for the season.**

I cannot stress enough how important it is to get your figures right from the start. Once you have introduced yourself and agreed your rates with your first client, this will be more or less the rate that you'll have to charge throughout the season. Next year, of course, you can review your prices and set them higher in line with your costs.

Charging enough

The main reason that gardeners come and go so quickly in this sector of the business is that they haven't charged enough. All too late they realise that they're earning less than if they were sitting at the checkout of their local supermarket. Despondency creeps in and they quickly come to regret ever starting their round and there it ends. Everyone loses. The clients, many of whom would have been willing to pay more had they been asked, no longer have a gardener, and the gardener no longer has a business.

Undercharging is an easy mistake to make. Don't ever underestimate your costs. Carry out as much research as you can before offering an hourly rate.

Getting started

You'll need to:

- Define the geographical area you are intending to cover.

- Make this area as small as you possibly can. Time travelling between clients is earning time lost.

- Be clear from the beginning on what your service does and doesn't include.

- Not be put off if the competition is charging less. They may not be offering the same service. If they are, then they may not be insured. Finally, if you really believe that they are offering everything you are at a cheaper rate – good luck to them. Remember there are only so many clients they can manage to get around. Eventually, probably much sooner than you think, they will become fully booked and what they charge will no longer be an issue.

Good news spreads fast

Good, reliable gardeners are very hard to find. Believe me! As soon as you've gardened for a number of clients word will spread and soon you'll have calls from friends of your existing clients all asking for your help. It's a great boost to your ego. From then on it's relatively easy to plan your days and weeks. Initially, you may have to change a few appointments around so that you can group your clients into areas. My experience has been that the public are more than happy to be flexible and accommodate you, provided you inform them in advance and try not to make any further changes.

Pre-launch checklist

Here's a checklist of what you'll need to do, or at least consider, prior to starting.

- Get a large, page-a-day diary.
- Define what service you're going to provide.
- Write an inventory of all your tools, and decide if you need any new ones and if so, if you have enough money to buy them.
- Get some advertising cards printed.
- Arrange indemnity insurance.
- Register with the Inland Revenue as being self-employed.
- Get a map of your local area.
- Decide on a name for your business.
- Decide how much you are going to charge per hour.
- Decide if you are going to have a minimum charge.
- Work out how much time you are able to spend actually gardening. From this work your diary into available slots.
- Remember to record all your business expenditure before you start. You must get, and keep, all receipts.
- Have a system for recording the work you do for your clients.

Coping with the paperwork

Keep it simple.

Even the smallest of gardening rounds will require some basic administration systems if you are to be successful.

Personal computers

Nothing fancy is required. If you have a personal computer you may wish to keep your systems on your hard drive. But make sure you maintain a back-up disk in case your system crashes and you lose your information.

Manual systems

My own personal preference is to keep my client records on a manual record card system. The main advantage of doing it this way is you don't first have to turn your PC on if all you want to do is find a telephone number. Whether you decide to computerise your records or maintain a manual system is very much down to your personal preference. But whatever you do, make sure you keep records.

The most basic administration system should include the following:

- client record cards
- work schedules
- page-a-day diary
- inventory
- machinery service and repair log
- bookkeeping system.

Client record cards

The simplest method of keeping client records is to purchase a medium sized index record card system. Most high street stationers sell them. Record cards are filed alphabetically. You create one card for each of your clients and include the following information:

- name and address
- telephone number
- the day and time you plan to visit them
- frequency of visits – weekly, fortnightly or once a month
- brief description of the weekly tasks that your client requires you to carry out
- any special requirements for plant care
- hourly rate.

It's important that you begin as you mean to go on and give each new client a record card. You can also create a provisional record card for clients whom you are about to visit but have not as yet agreed to hire your services.

Don't be tempted to keep all your records in one of those computerised data banks, or worse, your mobile phone.

I know a gardener who did this only to end up one night being thrown by his drunken friends fully clothed into the sea. Not only was his computer destroyed, but also his client records.

Work schedule

Again you will need to create a work schedule for each client.

The system I used when I ran my gardening round was to record all the weekly tasks that had to be done at the top of the page. Then I wrote a brief note of what I'd managed to do and when, followed by any reminders of work that was coming up in the future that I needed to prepare for, or perhaps allocate some extra time to. Here's an example:

CLIENT WORK SCHEDULE

Client	Mrs Williamson
Address	2 Tree Cottage, Rustington Road, West Sussex
Telephone number	00000123
Frequency	Every Monday morning, 9 – 11am (2hrs)
Required	Lawn cut. Weed and tidy borders, sweep paths
Special requirements	Prune fruit trees

WORK LOG

Date	Brief description of what you did

Pre-planned maintenance

Your schedule should include a section for forward planning. During your weekly visits you will need to adopt what is known as **pre-planned maintenance strategy**, which is basically a flash name for making sure that you're aware of what needs doing – and when!

By planning your work in advance you can ensure that you achieve everything that's required of you and also advise your client of when you will need to do some extra hours to cover the additional work.

Unsurprisingly, spring and autumn are the two seasons when you will you will need to allocate some extra hours to nearly all of your clients if you are stay on top of things.

The way I did this was to book a day's work with each of my clients. Or more than a day, if the garden was particularly large, or had much in the way of high maintenance shrubbery.

Although this will involve your clients paying out additional money to you at these times, they will, if you explain fully to those who are non-gardeners appreciate that you care enough to devote extra time to their garden. During autumn this is also a very useful way of earning a bit extra to cover you for the coming quiet season. While in spring it's great to start off your business with a decent cash injection.

Beware of setting unrealistic objectives

When I first started my gardening round, clients told me how many hours they would require my services. But when I began to work out what they actually wanted me to do, it was often impossible to achieve this in the limited amount of time they were willing to hire me for. When I pointed this out to them, they either extended my hours to cover what needed to be done, or reduced the list of tasks so that I could achieve them in the time allocated. However, I could have avoided all the stress and strains had I first created a viable client work schedule and made sure that I could do what I was being asked to do.

Carrying out an initial survey of your client's garden

Prior to completing your client work schedule you will need to take a number of factors into consideration. Treat this exercise as a mechanic would when looking under the bonnet of your car to see what needs to be done. They won't say they can repair or service your vehicle until they first establish what they will have to do.

When you first start your business and meet your prospective clients, you will probably feel a bit awkward or maybe nervous. You'll definitely be keen to impress your client that you are the right person to look after their garden. This is fine. *Nothing wrong with some positive enthusiasm, but make sure that you spend a little time surveying your future garden.*

Pay particular attention to the following:

- What is the current condition of the garden?
- Is it well maintained?
- Or does it look as if it hasn't had any attention for many months if not years?
- Does it need extra work to bring it up to a manageable standard?
- How much pruning, hedge trimming and high maintenance shrubbery is in the garden?

- Are you going to be solely responsible for the upkeep and maintenance of the garden or is the owner intending to work in it to?
- If so, what work will he/she/they be undertaking?

Don't be afraid to ask your prospective client as many questions as you need answers.

> My experience has been that all my prospective clients have been more than happy to answer questions. And at the end of our meeting I've been able to say whether or not I could achieve what was being asked of me. There were times when I had to say to people that their garden was too large, too full of high-maintenance shrubs and trees for me to realistically undertake to keep it as it should be for two hours a week. This offended none. If anything I went up in their estimation as they could see that I wanted their garden to be as beautiful as it deserved to be.

Beware of non-gardeners

Non-gardeners who mistakenly believe that a beautiful garden can be achieved by simply hiring a gardener two hours a fortnight aren't uncommon. It's not their fault. They're not trying to rope you into working fewer hours so they can pay you less. They simply don't understand how time-consuming gardening can be.

I've had situations where I've been the sole gardener responsible for everything, including watering the plants and dead-heading seasonal bedding. Believe me it is simply not possible to keep a garden looking at its best when your clients insist on having lots of high-maintenance planting, and don't have any intention of even watering the grounds during the summer months!

You're heading for certain disaster when you agree to work for such clients if you don't first outline what is and more importantly isn't achievable during your regular visits.

Don't be afraid to say that what's being asked of you is impossible to achieve in the time given.

Keeping your diary

Make sure you buy a decent, hard-backed, day-to-a-page diary, as a well-organised diary is vital to your success.

Divide each day that you intend to work into hourly slots. Choose a start time, a break time and a finish time.

Work to a minimum charge

Although you are dividing your diary into hourly slots, you must never agree to garden for someone for just one hour, it's simply not economical. The minimum period you should book any client for is two hours, even if the work only takes you one-and-a-half hours.

Imagine that you visit our friends Mr and Mrs Garden. When you get there they show you around a relatively small patch of lawn with a perimeter bed running around it. They explain to you that as they're now getting on in years they would like someone to cut the lawn and weed the border for them every week. By now you've a fair idea of what you can achieve in an hour and you estimate that this garden will take you an hour a week tops. Okay? Now comes the important bit. They ask you how much it's going to cost them. You don't tell them two hours (let's say your hourly rate is £10), which will be £20. Instead you tell them that while you appreciate that theirs is a relatively small garden, your minimum charge is £20.

I did this when I ran my gardening round and it worked very well.

Economies of scale

Most businesses have a minimum charge, although generally we're unaware of this. You can't walk into a supermarket, select a packet of biscuits from the shelf, open it and take one to the counter. Just as you can't choose how much milk you buy other than the pre-packed quantities. This is because of what is known as economies of scale. This grand economical theory simply means that in order for the product to be produced at a certain price, it must be sold in a certain quantity to make it profitable.

While we are not selling a product we are selling a service. It's important that:

◆ You see every available hour as a commodity.
◆ You sell at a certain price if you are to remain in business.
◆ You have a minimum price. The secret is not to tell your clients this. I'm not advocating that you do anything underhand, only be aware of what can happen if you say too much.

To illustrate my point this is what happened to me one Friday afternoon.

Case study

I was just finishing up for one of my regular clients when their neighbour raised her head above the garden fence and asked me if I could come and remove a bush from her garden. 'It's only a small one,' she said. 'Shouldn't take you too long.'

I was tired. It had been a long day and a long week and all I really wanted to do was tidy up, go home and dive into a nice refreshing shower. But here was an opportunity to earn more, so what the heck. I agreed to come and have a look.

'What is it?' I asked trying to figure out what this green bush was.

'Dunno,' she said, 'a friend gave it to me a few years ago and she'd no idea what it was either. No one since has been able to identify it.'

'And you want it out?'

'Yes, I hate it. It's got to go.'

I'd estimated that it would take me around ten minutes at the most. So I quoted £15.

'Great,' she said. 'Would you like a tea?'

Sounded good. But I wasn't going to be there that long. 'No thanks I'm fine.' And off I went setting about digging this bush out.

To this day, I still don't know what it was, but whatever it was, it didn't want to come out. The roots seemed to reach to hell and back. My increasing sense of frustration wasn't helped by my new client's insistence on providing a continual running commentary describing her extensive gardening knowledge, interrupted occasionally to introduce some bit of family history.

I yanked, pushed and pulled, dug and cut and when I finally felt it giving way, my spade snapped.

'Oh dear,' my client said. And off she went on a lengthy outpouring of how new tools were not as good as old tools and how she didn't want to sound clever, but when she saw my spade she did think that particular make wasn't really the best choice a gardener could make.

I was just seconds away from throttling her when I finally managed to remove the bush.

'Great,' she said.

By the time I'd loaded the bush into the back of my trailer, tidied away my tools including my now useless spade, I had been there just over 40 minutes. I was exhausted. But then came the bombshell.

'You couldn't help me move those pots around, could you?'

I looked to where a row of heavy-looking, terracotta pots stood filled with soil. There was no way, even if I had wanted, that I could have managed to muster up the strength let alone enthusiasm to lift one of these giants.

'I'm sorry,' I said trying to sound patient and polite. 'But I really do have to be going.'

'Oh,' she said looking at her watch. 'But you've only been here for just over a half hour.'

Obviously through speaking with her neighbour she had known my hourly rate was £10. Therefore she'd assumed that I would be with her for an hour and a half. Clearly, she was keen on getting value for money. I politely told her that my minimum charge was normally £20, but that I had reduced it on this occasion. Why? I don't know.

The whole job was a difficulty from start to finish. I broke my favourite spade, nearly did my back in and had a huge bush in the back of my trailer that would cost me money to dump, and all for £15. Replacing the spade alone cost me £24.

Make sure you decide on your minimum price and that you stick to it, and

Don't ever apologise for charging a fair price.

The secret of a successful diary

You will need to run your diary in much the same way as a dentist or doctor would by allocating set appointments. Divide up your day into slots of no less than two hours. This is the smallest slot you can realistically sell. *Anything less than two hours simply isn't worth it.* But then what will you do if a friend of one of your existing clients, who lives near to them, asks for your help with their garden, but what they want done will take less than an hour? This is where your minimum charge comes in. Under such circumstances you can explain that you have a minimum charge. This worked for me and I found that people understood. If you do come across someone who starts dividing your hourly rate into segments and then telling you how much they'll be willing to pay you, my advice is for you to politely leave. Don't waste any more of your time.

Create and maintain an inventory list

Whatever business you decide to run you will need to keep a list of all your equipment and tools.

I keep my inventory in an A4 ring binder. The information I record is as follows:

Item	Date acquired	Cost	Guarantee expiry date
Lawn Mower	7 May 200X	£460	6 May 200X
Spade	5 June 200X	£25	Lifetime (DIY store)

Keeping your records updated is vital for a number reasons.

- You have an accurate record of your capital expenditure.

- Each year you can offset a percentage of this expenditure, usually 25%, against tax.

- Over a period of time you can see which equipment regularly needs replacing and at what cost. This is essential for cost planning and cash flow forecasting.

- Recording the date when the item's guarantee expires is essential to ensuring you take advantage of such guarantees. If the item is not performing as it should be then you should return it and either have it repaired or replaced. When your business expands, it's difficult to remember when you purchased certain pieces of equipment.

- If you are unfortunate enough to suffer a break-in, or have your tools destroyed in some other way, your insurance company will need to see an inventory.

Create and maintain a service and repair log

At some point in the future your equipment will need servicing, if only a good clean and oiling. Similar to the inventory, by maintaining accurate records you can ensure that you keep your tools and machinery in good order.

You'll need to record:

- the dates the item has been serviced and the date of the next service
- the cost of servicing
- who carried out the service
- any relevant comments.

If you are to make your business as profitable as possible, then you must keep a close eye on costs. Servicing costs are one such cost that creep up on you without you realising. Then there is the cost of you losing the item for a day, week or however long it takes to have it repaired. Unless you're one of the few fortunate enough to carry out your own servicing you will have to take it to an authorised dealer. Depending on where you live this could involve a time-consuming journey and don't be surprised if they tell you it won't be ready for a week. Imagine the impact losing your mower will have on your gardening round.

> Try to book your equipment in for servicing when you yourself are planning to be on holiday. That way you lessen down time and improve overall profitability.

Forward planning is essential. By keeping a log you can foresee when your equipment will require servicing and book it in well in advance, thus ensuring as little down-time as possible.

Bookkeeping

Whatever type of business you decide on you will have to keep records of your income and expenditure. This is a legal requirement. You must keep records for at least five years from the latest date for sending back your tax return.

Chapter 7 looks at bookkeeping in greater detail, but for the moment you need to know that in order to satisfy the Inland Revenue or other official body, you accounts must be a true and honest reflection of your business. *You must keep an accurate record of all your business expenditure and income.* Without receipts you will find it virtually impossible to substantiate your expenditure.

> Keep all receipts whether you think you need them or not.

Limitations of a gardening round

Is a gardening round really for you?

As a business I no longer offer the services as a gardening round. There were a number of reasons why I had to close my round. The deciding factor for me was that my gardening round was incapable of supporting me through those long winter months.

While many businesses such as hotels, guesthouses, seaside arcades and so on close for the winter, their earnings are likely to be far higher than those of a self-employed gardener. My own personal financial circumstances meant that I couldn't afford to close for three months of the year, much as I was tempted to.

You may well find that many of your clients want you to work for them throughout the winter months. Indeed, there are lots of jobs to be getting on with in the garden during this period.

During the winter short days mean shorter earning periods

The main draw-back is the short days. This means that the average hours you can work in the garden is about six. That's if it's not too wet or snowing or everywhere is under a few feet or inches of water.

If you've enough regular clients to see you through these bleak months, remember that your working hours will be severely reduced, and with it, your earnings.

By adjusting your cash flow forecasts to cover seasonal downturns, you can ensure that even though your income is reduced, you are financially prepared for it.

Summary

1. A gardening round can provide a good income, provided it's set up and run correctly.

2. Here's a low cost start-up opportunity that's easy and fun to operate.

3. Reliability is often more important to your clients than being the best gardener in the world. You'd don't have to be a wizard at every aspect of gardening in order to start here, but you must be willing to learn new things and listen to what your clients tell you.

4. Make sure you set prices to allow enough return to make the commitment worthwhile.

Ten ways of ensuring that your gardening round is a success

1. Get your pricing right from day one and make sure that you include an element of profit in your calculations.

2. Buy the best tools that you can.

3. Keep them well maintained and always in serviceable condition.

4. Have adequate insurance in place from day one.

5. Keep your round as geographically tight as possible, thus reducing travelling time between appointments.

6. You'll need to do all-round gardening if you are to enjoy this business and make a complete success of it. Therefore read as many gardening books as you can and never stop learning.

7. Plan to take your holidays outside of the main gardening season.

8. Decide now what you are going to do for the winter months. If you're planning to stay open, work out some financial forecasts and make sure that you can cover your survival income during this time.

9. Continually monitor the costs of providing your service and make sure that your pricing takes into consideration any significant changes.

10. Always do what you say, and if you're unable to for whatever reason, make sure that you keep your client informed and updated.

Never apologise for charging a fair price.

CHAPTER 4

The General Gardening Business

Gardening is the greatest business in the world.

The inner workings of a general gardening business

When I stuck my first card in a newsagent's window, I never imagined that my business would grow into what it is today – a full-scale gardening/landscaping business.

This is an all-year-round business where potential earnings are excellent and the satisfaction of running this operation is enormous.

There is nothing routine about this business. You'll have to:

◆ continually think on your feet
◆ be capable of running a number of different projects at any one time.
◆ manage and motivate a workforce, even if it's only you
◆ work to budgets
◆ accurately produce written quotes and estimates
◆ become an all-round expert.

> **It's not always easy and there is no guarantee of success.**

You'll have to be comfortable with uncertainty, and able to motivate yourself when others would have given up and got a proper job.

But the rewards can be enormous. Nothing quite compares to the satisfaction that finishing a new garden brings, the sheer pleasure of seeing a new, beautiful garden occupying an area that prior to your arrival was overgrown, unsightly and unusable.

What does it for me is at the end of a job to see the pleasure that my finished work brings to others.

Surely there can be no better way to earn your living than making people happy?

Specific jobs at agreed prices

This business concentrates on quoting for specific jobs, agreeing a price, carrying out the work and moving on. It's a fun, fast-moving, hectic working schedule, which brings enormous rewards. To run this business successfully, you must be able to have lots of things on the go at any one time and not be flustered by it.

Some services offered by a general gardening business

There is no limit to the diversity of services that you offer. You're only limited by your imagination, and perhaps in the early days your experience.

Start slowly

My own opinion is that anyone contemplating this type of operation should start slowly. It's best to establish your business by offering a quality service based on what you know now, ie your current expertise, and expand your range of services when your experience and capital allow.

Listed below are the services I offer as part of my business. This isn't a definitive list as we're introducing new services all the time.

- general garden maintenance
- overgrown gardens cleared
- new gardens created
- existing garden makeovers
- fencing erected and repaired
- areas redesigned and replanted
- tree stump removal
- hard features created
- water features created
- greenhouses erected and repaired
- herb gardens created
- turfing

- lawn care advice and consultancy
- coaching
- garden planning/design service.

Tree surgery – a cautionary note

The sheer number of general gardening companies that include 'tree surgery' among their list of services never ceases to amaze me.

Arboriculture, the care and maintenance of trees, is a business in itself. This is a specialist area where you must have proper training before you embark on any work.

- You will find that your general landscape gardening Public Liability Insurance will not cover you for tree work. You can of course, for an additional fee, extend your cover to include tree felling and tree care, but don't be surprised when your insurance company asks for proof of your qualifications.

- The initial costs of providing this service are also prohibitive as not only will you have to spend a considerable amount on cutting equipment, but you will also have to have some form of tree chipping/shredding unit. These will cost you anything from £8,000 upwards. Plus you'll also have to have a suitable vehicle in which to accommodate the chippings.

Unless you are qualified in this type of work, my advice is that you would do well to steer clear of it. If you would like to work in this field then you will need to apply to your local agricultural college and gain the necessary training to do the job professionally.

Begin by offering services that you can easily provide both in terms of:

- experience/expertise
- financial outlay.

There are a number of services on this list that can be tackled without having to rely on years of gardening experience. For example, there are many people who need help clearing out an old, overgrown garden prior to them constructing a new one. This sort of work calls for more in the way of physical strength than gardening expertise and for the newcomer this is a relatively safe way to begin. Provided you offer a competitive, reliable service you will find that running your business on this basis alone can be relatively profitable.

Then expand and become more specialised

However, if you are to truly shine and reach your full potential you will undoubtedly at some point in the future wish to *expand your business by offering wider services.*

Some of the work we now do is quite specialised. Few landscaping companies offer to design and build herb gardens, which is surprising as with the ever-increasing interest in organic and natural gardening, knowledge of herbs and how to create a beautiful garden using these wonderful plants is very much in demand.

Likewise few businesses offer a gardening coaching service, yet how many people as soon as they hear you're a keen gardener or someone who runs their own gardening business will ask you for advice on the most elementary of subjects? Every month of the year thousands of people across the country move into their first homes that have a garden and their quest for knowledge begins. There are books to read, night classes to attend and so on, but nothing comes close to having a knowledgeable, friendly gardener come to your own garden to teach you the ropes.

This business is run in much the same way as driving instruction. You can either offer set lessons, following a pre-agreed syllabus, or simply one-off sessions coaching a certain area.

> **Successful garden coaching depends on your ability to get on with people and make them feel at ease.**

Spending your days working in gardens can be physically exhausting. Therefore you need a sense of balance in your work. This is why I would encourage you, when planning this type of business, to offer either one or preferably a number of services that are not too physically demanding such as gardening coaching, gardening planning, greenhouse erection and so on.

If you feel your knowledge is lacking in a particular area of gardening then you should invest time and money in furthering your education. I love going on short courses. Not only do I find them really useful in terms of learning how to do something, but I also enjoy the social side of meeting people, getting to hear others' views and opinions and making new friends.

Garden planning

With the recent avalanche of telly programmes featuring garden makeovers, naturally all and sundry are now out advertising their services as garden designers.

Do you need a formal qualification to design a garden?

The simple answer is no you don't. You can start advertising your services as a garden designer, tomorrow if you so wish.

However, you would be well advised not to. Lots of people these days are calling themselves garden designers, when really they are anything but. You must have some form of training in this area before you start messing about with other people's gardens. There is a lot more to designing a garden than simply deciding where to put the pre-built water feature.

Train to be a designer

Some years ago I took a night class in garden design at my local college. I thoroughly enjoyed the course and learnt so much not just about design, but also ways of overcoming common problems, and of course how to think like a designer.

Oddly enough, many professionally qualified designers are not gardeners in their own right. They freely admit that their area of expertise is the creation of a garden that satisfies their client's brief as opposed to dwelling too much on the ins and outs of gardening craft.

I offer a garden planning service as opposed to a design service.

Here's a summary of what it entails:

- Carrying out an initial visit to the garden and making a survey.
- Discussing with my clients what they want from their garden and how much they are willing to spend on achieving it. This is what's known as completing a 'client brief'.
- Once the budget is agreed, I have enough information to work out an initial design, which I then discuss with my clients.
- If they're happy with my ideas, I work on a finished design. If not, then I have a greater understanding of their requirements and I come up with a fresh design.
- I then present my final design together with an estimate of the costs involved, and timescales for completion.
- The final stage is building the actual garden.

I also build gardens from other garden designers' plans.

One stop shop

The main advantage of my service is that potential clients only have to negotiate with the one company throughout the project, and in doing so we can quickly amend and adjust the original idea to suit any changing needs.

Working to your client's design
Something that is becoming increasing popular is clients who wish to design their own garden and employ a landscaping company to do all the work.

If you get offered such an assignment you must make sure that what you have been asked for is achievable in terms of both building the garden and how much your client is willing to pay.

Beware of plans that are too ambitious

Regrettably, many of the gardening design programmes on the television fail to give any indication of what the finished garden is going to cost. Often the costs incurred in creating these gardens probably exceed the value of the house. Bringing in heavy-duty cranes to lift boulders and gigantic concrete supports over the roof of a two-storey semi doesn't come cheap. Neither does the cost of hiring a specially adapted low loader to take stones the size of those at Stonehenge from a quarry in the north of the country all the way to London. Costs like these are enormous.

> **Prior to undertaking any project you must ensure that all the costs have been agreed and your client is aware of how much the whole thing is likely to cost.**

Let your experience work for you

Experienced gardeners have lots to offer when it comes to planning a garden. At some time you will have experienced the difficulties of working in a poorly planned garden.

◆ Gardens where the lawn has been laid right up to the patio, which is about six inches higher than the lawn.

◆ Lawns that are surrounded by kerbing, or worse are butted right up to a wall.

◆ Anywhere you have to use a strimmer because you cannot fit your lawnmower demonstrates bad planning.

Soon you'll be visiting and working in all sorts of different gardens. Some will become your favourites simply because they're a pleasure to work in. Others will of course become your worst nightmare and you'll constantly berate yourself for not charging more. It never ceases to amaze me just how much extra work is created as a result of bad planning.

Don't be afraid to offer a garden planning service. However, actual garden design is best left to those who've undertaken the training. Of course, there is nothing to stop you from training to be a garden designer. Many of the colleges now offer distance learning courses, which means you can study in the comfort of your own home in the evenings without encroaching too much on your work. Course fees are from about £400 upwards and normally are legitimate costs to your business and can therefore be tax deductible.

> **Don't limit your business to offering one service. While this approach is okay initially, as a long-term strategy you will find your business getting stuck in a rut.**

Getting started

Starting this type of business requires more in the way of capital than working a gardening round.

Start by making a list of the services that you are planning to offer. It doesn't matter whether you have all the tools necessary to do these jobs or not, make your list anyway.

Now consider what you will need in terms of the following:

◆ What tools are you going need to buy before you can start?
◆ Work out roughly how much this is going to cost.

Capital

You possibly need some money available to you to set up your business. This will depend on what tools and equipment you already have available.

You will also need some money available to your business to cover your day-to-day expenditure. This is known as **working capital.**

> How much you need will depend on your personal circumstances. Ideally you should have about three months' survival income tucked up in a high interest savings account.

Start-up costs

These may include funding one or all of the following:

- tools
- vehicle
- insurance cover
- initial training.

Tools

Buy the best quality tools that you can afford, and only those that you will use regularly, and never buy large expensive items such as cultivators or heavy-duty chippers. These are best hired for specific jobs. Buying them and having them sitting in your shed or garage unused is similar to having money in a bank account that doesn't pay you interest.

Hiring equipment

I hire the following equipment regularly and would never dream of buying any of them regardless of price.

- all-terrain lawnmowers
- towable wood chipper
- stump grinder
- turf cutter
- cement mixer
- heavy duty post hole borer

- mini diggers
- power barrows.

All of these tools would cost a lot of money to purchase and, even if my business were cash-rich enough to afford them, the cost of ensuring they are kept well-maintained and serviced is too great.

Hiring is an excellent way of acquiring the equipment you want, when you want it, without having to shell out loads of cash and worry when it's next due for a service.

Don't be afraid to negotiate on brochure rates

I have found all of the major tool hiring companies, and many of the smaller ones, more than happy to negotiate on hiring fees, that is as soon as I tell them that I am hiring as a business as opposed to a private renter. Hiring companies understand better than anyone that Mr Private renter will not be hiring a turf cutter in December, when you most likely will need one. So make sure that you negotiate some sensible trade prices with your supplier and don't be afraid to shop around.

When hiring any equipment you should:

- Always ensure that the equipment you are being given appears to be well maintained and in a safe condition. If the recent findings by the Trading Standards are anything to go by, not all equipment from hire agents including some of the big players, is as safe as it could be, particularly gardening equipment such as hedge trimmers.

- Ask for a demonstration before you take possession of the equipment. Most hire companies will do this automatically, but when you're a 'trade customer' many will assume that you already know how to use the equipment.

- Get a copy of as many tool hire catalogues and price lists as you can.

- If some are unwilling to offer you any discount don't tell them that unless they do that you won't do any business with them. There will be days when your favoured supplier does not have what you require in stock!

- Make sure you are clear about who is liable in the event that the equipment is damaged or stolen. You may find that the trade price being offered to you means that the hire company expects you to cover the tool on your business insurance.

- Read any agreement carefully before you sign it.

- Remember that most companies charge extra for on-site delivery and collection of the tool.

- If you're working alone, ensure that one person can operate the item you're planning to hire.

- When pricing a specific job always make sure that you include the extra hire companies charges, which aren't always initially apparent – items such as insurance, additional safety gear, grinding disks, blades etc.

The hire company may require you to produce evidence of your professional competency when hiring certain items of equipment, for example chain saws. Some of the larger tool hire companies offer short courses in how to use equipment correctly and safely.

Purchasing tools – some more guidelines

- Buy the best you possibly can.

- Buy from recognised dealers as opposed to DIY stores. Most dealers will be happy to negotiate on prices and offer a far better after-sales service than DIY or retail stores. If there is a problem with equipment that is under warranty, and they have sold it to you, dealers are far more likely to lend you replacement equipment while your own is being repaired.

- Discuss with the sales person what you want the equipment for. There's no point in telling them you want a lawnmower to cut lawns. Tell them how many hours a day, week, month you're expecting to run the machine for and ask them to suggest the most suitable machine.

◆ There is nothing wrong with buying secondhand equipment provided you buy from a reputable dealer. Don't be temped to save money by buying from an unknown source. Not only could the equipment be stolen, but also you have no guarantee that it'll do the job you require safely and efficiently.

◆ Where possible only purchase petrol-driven tools. Electrical tools aren't much good when you have nowhere to plug them in and are next to useless in wet conditions.

◆ Plan all your purchases carefully. Do you really need it? Will you use it sufficiently to make it pay? Are you better off hiring it?

> **Tools represent a substantial part of your initial outlay – buy only what you're going to use regularly not everything you think you need.**

There will always be something that you could buy for your business. However strong the temptation may be to rush out and buy whatever item this may be, resist it. Nothing is worse than having some expensive, un-used item gradually deteriorating into a rust bucket in some corner of your garage. Every item should be earning its keep in your business. If not then it should be sold as quickly as possible.

> **Every item must earn its place in your business. If not, then you must dispose of it while it still has a resale value.**

Introducing a tool replacement programme

One thing is definite – they won't last forever. Therefore you need to plan a tool replacement programme.

Unfortunately, a consequence of starting a business from scratch is that generally you will buy all you need to start in one swoop right at the beginning. Of course by doing it this way you should be in a good position to negotiate a good discount. However, the down side is that all your warranties will expire at the same time, and depending on the type of equipment and what it's used for, you may find that servicing and replacement dates for your equipment all happen at one time. You need to avoid this. The last thing you want to have to do is replace all of your equipment in one go, or fork out to have it all serviced at the same time. The downtime alone would cripple any business, let alone the bills.

> **Make sure you trade in your existing tools against either new or quality used tools when they still have some life left in them. Don't ever run your equipment until it has no re-sale value.**

In order to reduce the burden of replacing your equipment you should:

◆ Give each tool a realistic lifespan in your business.

◆ From this work out a replacement schedule based on the anticipated lifespan of the item. Try to replace equipment like lawnmowers at the end of the season as opposed to the beginning, so that you can take advantage of discounts and sale prices.

◆ Gradually trade-up your existing or start-off equipment, to buy something more suitable. This way you phase in new or used equipment (you can get some excellent deals from dealers on used equipment, as your budget will allow).

Similarly, you can forecast when your equipment will need servicing, and you should build a budget into your monthly cash flow forecast to accommodate this expenditure.

Remember that most expenditure can be foreseen, provided you spend sufficient time preparing a replacement and maintenance schedule. Believe me, it will be time well spent.

Periodically, say every three months, or at least every quarter, you should go through your equipment inventory:

◆ Are the tools you have suitable for your needs?

◆ Can you dispose of those that you are not using, or are unsuitable for your business?

◆ What tools do you still need? Judge need on the basis of what a particular tool would do for your business in terms of both producing additional revenue and reducing time spent on current jobs. For example, if you're currently cutting hedges using clipping shears (there's nothing wrong with this, and many of your clients may welcome this approach), by purchasing a petrol driven hedge trimmer would this mean that you could cut more hedges per day, thereby increasing your revenue?

◆ Be brutal – if you don't need whatever it is that's clogging up your workshop/garage then sell it.

Find a reputable local machinery dealer

Finding a reliable dealer isn't always as easy as it sounds. If you're having problems then don't be afraid to ask those already in the trade who they use to supply them with their equipment. Or if you don't fancy doing this, pay a visit to your local hardware shop and ask them. I'm convinced that in every part of the country, no matter how isolated you may appear to be, tucked away somewhere you'll find a reputable dealer who'll be more than capable of servicing all your needs. All you have to do is find them!

The cost of initially acquiring, and then servicing the machinery necessary to run your business will make a fairly large hole in your pocket. You must spend wisely.

> You should only purchase capital equipment such as tools and the like as part of a carefully planned programme, and the costs of servicing this equipment should be adequately covered in your cash flow and profit and loss forecasts.

Vehicles

If you are going to have to buy a vehicle there are a number of factors that you will need to consider:

◆ available capital
◆ new or used
◆ type of business that you are intending to run
◆ insurance costs
◆ running costs.

Available capital

Put simply, how much money have you available to spend on a reliable, presentable vehicle for your business?

New or used?

I would say that anyone contemplating setting up a gardening business would be well advised not to purchase a new vehicle. By the very nature of the work that you will be doing, your vehicle is in for a bit of a pounding. You'll be out there working in all sorts of weathers, tackling all kinds of jobs that generate a generous helping of mud and sweat, not to mention rotting foliage, compost and all the rest, which means that very soon your shiny new van, pick-up or whatever you bought won't look so good. And if you've acquired the vehicle on some sort of a vehicle lease scheme, you may be in for some heavy penalties when you return the vehicle at the end of the lease period.

My current van has been around the clock once and boasts over 120,000 miles. It's extremely reliable, very presentable and cost me a fraction of what I would have had to shell out had I bought a newer, lower mileage vehicle. A clean, professional image is vital to your business and you should therefore avoid anything that looks too tatty, but on the other hand you don't have to have something that's clean enough to carry food items.

> **My advice is that you should choose a used, reliable vehicle. Make sure whatever you buy is mechanically sound. Get either a local mechanic or the AA or RAC to check it out for you if you're not sure what to look for. Provided the bodywork is presentable and the vehicle capable of meeting the requirements of your business, you'll be able to pick up a suitable vehicle for a fraction of the cost of a new one.**

Make sure that what you buy is what you need

What type of business you're intending to run will determine the type of vehicle most suitable for your needs.

◆ If lawn-cutting is to be a major part of your operation then you will need something that is capable of taking your lawnmowers, grass cuttings etc. You may find a high-sided trailer with a loading ramp more suitable than a van.

◆ If your business will involve taking regular amounts of garden debris to the dump you'll need a vehicle that will take as much volume as possible.

The sort of debris that I have to remove in my business tends to be hedge trimmings and the like. Usually my loads are very light, but bulky.

You may need to consider some form of chipper/shredder for transforming bulky waste into smaller quantities, thus saving on tipping fees.

My own vehicle arrangements include a van and a high-sided trailer. One very much complements the other.

Insurance costs

We're now living in a world dominated by call centres, where 'customer services' amounts to little more than a question and answer session over the phone. If you don't have all the answers, you don't get your quote. How an insurance company expects you to the know the registration of the vehicle you intend to purchase when as yet you haven't found one is beyond me.

To add to my frustrations the vast majority of the companies that I phoned up told me they didn't do commercial van insurance, and this after wasting time in a lengthy queue.

Find a good insurance broker

Before you buy any vehicle you should phone your broker and get a quote. I'm a fan of insurance brokers ever since I spent a wasted morning phoning around trying to get some insurance quotes.

Get your insurance broker to do the legwork for you. My broker couldn't be more helpful and is more than happy to get all the quotes I need, whenever I need them, and without knowing the registration number.

The cost of commercial vehicle insurance varies enormously depending on the type of vehicle you are planning to insure. I managed to get a fairly substantial discount on my insurance simply because my vehicle is older. This suits me fine!

Running costs

- insurance
- fuel
- tax
- servicing and MOT
- tyres.

There's no doubt that fuel prices will forever be on the increase. Therefore it's important that you buy something that's as economical as possible to run, especially if you plan to cover a large area.

Whatever vehicle you choose make sure it's capable of doing the job you want it to do. Too small and you'll be forever trying to compromise. Too big and it'll cost you a fortune to run.

> By having your vehicle tastefully sign-written with your company name and telephone number, you can greatly reduce the amount of money you have to spend on advertising.

Financing your business

The positive cash flow effect

In Chapter 1, we looked at what market place our future businesses would be likely to operate in, and I said that I believe the domestic is the best one to tackle first. The main reason for this is that you will have what is often referred to as a 'cash business', one where your clients settle their accounts as soon as the job is completed.

This means that you won't have to wait for months for your money, which is good news for your cash flow, thus creating **positive cash flow**.

However, this doesn't mean that you'll be earning your target income from week one, or possibly even year one. As with all business, things take time to develop. During this initial development period you will need enough money available to cover:

◆ your personal survival income
◆ your business running costs.

Of course you may be very lucky and your circumstances may be such that you don't need much survival income and you have estimated that your running costs are going to be near zero. But if you're like I was when I first started, and had too many bills and not enough cash, then you will need to work out how you're going to have enough *working capital* available to tide you over what may initially be a financially difficult period.

Working capital can come from a number of sources:

- savings
- a loan
- other income.

Other income could be anything from renting out your spare room to taking a paid part-time job. *Try to have at least three months' survival income available to you before you start.* If you don't have it, then you could consider starting your business as a part-time operation while keeping your main job. This way you can save enough money to enable you to go full time at some later date, hopefully in the not too distant future.

From experience I can tell you that nothing is worse than whittling away the early hours of the morning lying awake worrying about how you are going to make ends meet, when you should really be resting preparing for another hectic day.

Obtaining funding for your business

If you're planning to approach a bank for finance you will have to have a well thought-out business plan with which to impress them. But don't despair if they won't lend you any money.

> During my presentation my bank manager appeared to be very enthusiastic about my ideas. But did he give me an overdraft? No. I had what I believed to be a fairly sound business plan. I had over £40,000 equity available in my property, which I was willing to let the bank have a charge on if they felt they needed to. I had an excellent credit history and had never had as much as a letter warning me I was overdrawn. But when the day came and the moment arrived the bank would not give me any credit. I still managed to start my business and as soon as I was well enough established I changed banks.
>
> When the bank told me I couldn't have an overdraft I was stuck. I had no way of financing my business other than to put my initial capital expenditure on a credit card. While this method isn't really to be recommended as the best way of starting your enterprise, it did work for me. In the first few months I put all my major expenditure on my credit card, which I then began to pay back from earnings. In a way it's more flexible than a bank overdraft as you have some control over how much you pay back each month. However, this is not to be recommended. I would advise you to avoid taking this route if possible. I know of at least one case where someone did this and the results were disastrous.

Clearly the best way of financing your business is to have enough cash in the bank without having to borrow at all. But if you don't, and you want to start, then you'll need to look at all the different ways of financing your new venture.

◆ Bank loan.

◆ Bank overdraft.

◆ Loan from another source.

◆ Income from another source, for example selling something you already have in order to finance your venture.

◆ Using your credit card to finance some or all of your initial essential purchases.

> **Whatever you do you must keep borrowing to a minimum.**

Alternatively, you could find ways of reducing the amount of money you need to have available by offering only those services that you can offer without any need for further capital expenditure. This is probably the most sensible approach, however it does mean that your business may initially comprise you cycling round your area clipping hedges using clipping shears. If this is what you have to do, then do it. There's nothing wrong with this approach. And as soon as money starts flowing into your business you could start expanding your services.

Sales and marketing launching strategy

We look at sales and marketing and ways of launching your businesses in more depth in Chapter 6. The time that you're planning to start your business will determine when you should begin your pre-launch strategy. If you're planning to start almost immediately, or have already begun, then you should have a look at Chapter 6 now to give you some ideas and help with planning a sales and marketing strategy that will make starting your business as painless as possible.

Getting the business – quotes and estimates

You will always be actively looking for new clients.

One important difference between running a general gardening business and a gardening round is that, with the latter, you will quickly achieve a regular client base and will arrive at the point where you no longer need to advertise or look for new customers. In running a general gardening business you will be constantly on the lookout for new clients, which is fun and exciting if tackled correctly.

The regulars

While undoubtedly you will have regular custom with this business, it will most probably be on a seasonal basis. Many of your clients will require you to carry out a pre-defined job on either an annual or bi-annual basis, for example a visit in spring to get the garden ready for the coming seasons, and the next visit in the autumn to tidy up and put the garden to bed for the winter. However, the vast majority of the work you do may be only one-off jobs. This means that *not only will you have to seek out new customers throughout the year, but you will also have to provide prospective clients with a written estimate* detailing how much the job they want doing is going to cost them.

The difference between a quote and an estimate

Estimate. Put simply an estimate is just what it says it is. It is an estimation of what you believe the job will cost to do. Of course the final bill can be greater or less than what you originally estimated. But unless there has been huge variations in the original work planned, then your final bill shouldn't vary too much from your original estimate.

Quotation. A quotation is much the same as an estimate in that you are providing your prospective client with how much you believe the job will cost to do. But there's one important difference:

If you provide your client with a quotation then generally the price quoted is the price you will have to charge. A quotation is a legally binding agreement, while an estimate is just that – an estimate.

Offer free estimates

My advice is that you offer free estimates, as opposed to free quotations. It's unlikely that you would either be able to or want to start charging for estimates and quotations. Were you to do this, I think it's a sure bet that few if any potential clients would ever agree to this. And who could blame them!

Visiting potential clients in their gardens and providing them with a written estimate is a major part of this business. The time it takes to do this properly should not be underestimated. Initially you may find some difficulty in trying to work out costings, especially when it comes to deciding how much you should be charging for labour. Unfortunately, there is no pre-determined formula that I can give you for arriving at your calculations. What follows is the method I use.

Estimate preparation

◆ Make a list of the jobs that you are being asked to provide an estimate for, or if it is only one job then still write it down.

◆ Now write down all the things that you will have to do in order to complete this job.

◆ Next put a rough estimate of how long you expect each individual task is likely to take you.

◆ Finally, list all the additional costs that you are likely to incur.

Case study

Here's an example of an estimate for cutting a front hedge.

My client, Mrs Welding, wants the hedge to be reduced in height by at least 2ft to allow additional light into her front garden. The hedge comprises mature, woody shrubbery, which will be difficult to cut.

Here is my list of the separate tasks that I will have to undertake. Alongside each in brackets I have roughly worked out how much time each task will take.

1. Cut the hedge (2.5 hours)
2. Clear up afterwards and put cuttings in trailer (1/2 hour)
3. Take debris to the dump (1/2 hour)

Additional costs will be as follows.

1. Tipping charge. I estimate the quantity of hedge trimmings, branches etc that I will have to remove will fill my trailer and any additional space I have in my van. The load will be bulky as opposed to heavy. Thus I'll be charged the minimum tipping charge – £24.

2. Fuel. Petrol for hedge trimmer and chain saw, and travelling to and from client's property, including tip.
Allow £10.
My hourly rate for hedge trimming is £15.
Thus my estimate is as follows.

Labour 4 hours x £15	£ 60
Tipping charge	£ 24
Fuel	£ 10
Total costs	£ 94
Plus 15% profit	£ 14.10
Final total	**£108**

Explanatory notes for my estimate

How did I arrive at £15 as being my hourly rate?

This is a relatively straightforward job, therefore I have charged my minimum hourly rate, this being £15. Were this task more difficult, for example if it involved more back-breaking work, I would increase my hourly rate accordingly and this could be anywhere between £15 and £40.

Tipping charges and fuel costs are self-explanatory.

Finally, I have included a 15% profit and rounded off the amount to give a final figure.

Get into good habits right from the beginning and always include, no matter how small, an element of profit.

This has nothing to do with greed or trying to milk as much as you can from your client. You include it because you are running a business and in doing so you are taking a risk. Not only is profit your return for investing your money and time in your business, but it's also necessary to cover the wear and tear on your equipment so that you can afford to buy new tools when needed.

Here's what my final written estimate to Mrs Welding would look like:

---

7 July 200X
Mrs J Welding
Lime Tree Cottage
Any Street
Sometown
BN1

Dear Mrs Welding

Thank you for asking me to provide you with an estimate for your proposed gardening work, which I understand to be as follows:

ESTIMATE

To cut and trim the entire front hedge, including side hedges, reducing the overall height by no less than 2 feet/610mm, remove all clippings and cuttings from site.

Labour and fuel	£84
Tipping charge	£24
Total estimated cost	£108

This estimate is valid for six weeks from the date of this letter.

If you would like to discuss this estimate or make an appointment to have the work done, then please do call me.

Yours sincerely
Paul Power
for Paul Power Landscapes

Don't be put off by having to provide written estimates. Initially you may find it somewhat daunting figuring out how much you should charge and whether or not you're too expensive or you haven't charged enough.

With experience you will soon learn how long certain jobs are likely to take you and the task of estimating will soon become easier.

Guidelines for estimate preparation

♦ During your initial meeting with your prospective client make sure that you take notes.

♦ Identify what exactly you are being asked to do. You'll find that some people you meet, whether deliberately or not, will be very vague about what they want done. You must clarify exactly what they want. If they want their hedges trimmed, fine. But how much do they want off the top? And get them to identify which hedge they want you to cut. Does the front include the sides? What about the back garden?

♦ Break down the job or jobs that you are being asked to do and decide how long they will take you. Be realistic. Quality work takes time.

♦ During your initial meeting, discuss with your client what the job will actually involve you doing.

♦ Point out that you are charged for dumping garden waste, and what those charges are. You may find that your client is happy for you to simply bag up the cuttings and that they will take them to the dump themselves. If this is the case then ensure that you remember to build in some additional labour to cover having to bag up the waste.

♦ If the job is such that you already know how much you are going to charge then tell your client during your initial meeting. If they say yes, they're happy with the price, then agree a provisional date to start, or if this is not available then agree on rough time scale.

♦ If you give a price straight away, always provide a written estimate too. By doing this there can be no argument at a later date as to what it was that you agreed you would do. Your estimate can also protect you from having to cope with unforeseen circumstances.

Unforeseen circumstances

There will be times when you will be asked to provide an estimate where the job appears to be relatively straightforward, such as digging over a border or removing a rockery and levelling the site. Both tasks are not difficult and you should have no problem providing your prospective client with an estimate.

Hidden hazards

However, what you would you do if when you start digging over the border you find your spade hits concrete and upon further investigation that the border isn't anything more than a light dressing of soil on top of what was a concrete patio? Or when removing the rockery you discover that it is covering up a coal bunker?

These scenarios are not uncommon. Neither is it always the case that your client has deliberately tried to mislead you. More often than not, it's simply that your client did not know whatever you found existed.

> When the unforeseen has happened to me it's usually been when I've been asked to work on a garden that the owner has recently acquired, and in all honesty they had no idea that there was a hidden patio, tree stump, concrete footpath, air raid shelter, or whatever. Fortunately, to-date all of my clients have been most understanding when I tell them that obviously removing the unforeseen obstacle will increase the price of the job.

It would be foolish to hope that you will always have such accommodating clients. Make sure that you cover this in your written estimate.

I strongly recommend that you include a short qualifying 'get out of trouble' paragraph in all your estimates:

'This estimate is based on the assumption that there are no hidden obstacles beneath the surface such as buried tree stumps, patios, hard core and the like. If such obstacles are found then the costs of removing them would be additional to those costs already described above.'

Provided you discuss these eventualities with your prospective clients during your initial meeting then there should be no problem if and when you come across the hidden patio. As I said earlier, I have had no problem with charging extra for dealing with the unforeseen. But it's good practice and a way of avoiding possible disputes to warn your client in advance that your price is based on the assumption that you're going to be digging over soil and not, as I've found on occasions, to first have to remove a footpath or patio!

Your estimate should be laid out in a way that is:

- easy to read
- unambiguous
- respectful, without being either patronising or grovelling
- clearly written, identifying what it is that you will be doing, in the event that your prospective client accepts your estimate.

Other issues you should cover

- measurements
- general notes.

When including any measurements, you must provide them in metric. There is no problem using feet and inches, provided you include the metric equivalent alongside. This is a legal requirement and not something that you can ignore.

You should also indicate how long your estimate is valid for. There is a good reason for this – your prospective client's garden will continue to grow until such time as they employ someone to do the work. Overgrown gardens became more overgrown as time goes on. This may mean that the job you initially thought would take you a half-day will now take a day. There will also be more cuttings, trimmings, weeds and so forth to take to the dump, which means increased tipping charges.

> **Estimates should only be valid for a set period and you should include this information in your written submission.**

Delivering your estimate

If you haven't already given any indication to your client of how much the job is likely to cost then you must be careful of just posting off your estimate and hoping for the best.

Wherever possible I try to give my client a price during my initial meeting with them. Obviously the more standard the job, the easier it should be for you to price there and then. By doing this I can get the order and book a date in the diary without having to worry about being undercut by the competition.

Standard jobs would include:

◆ hedge trimming
◆ lawn cutting
◆ weeding
◆ pruning.

These are the jobs that you should be able to give a price for there and then. *Bring your diary with you to the meeting so that as soon as you give your price you can book the work in. This isn't being pushy, this is being professional, and in my experience this is what clients are looking for.* Nothing is more frustrating than having to wait weeks for an estimate to arrive then to discover that you can't afford whatever it is you want done.

Initially, you may find it difficult to price jobs on the spot. This is only natural, but you'll soon become fluent at sizing up how long something is going to take you.

> I find it much easier to work out a price when I'm there looking at whatever it is I'm being asked to do as that way I can ask all the questions I need to as well as having a really good look at what the job will entail.

The jobs that you probably won't be able to quote for immediately would include:

◆ turfing
◆ creating hard features such as walls, pathways and patios
◆ large clearance jobs
◆ fencing.

Try to avoid posting your estimate without first discussing it with your clients.

Rather than simply post my estimate I like to talk it through with my clients. That way I am more likely to get the order than if I'd just posted it. So in the event that I'm unable to give a client a price at the initial meeting, I'll either try to arrange a second appointment, or if this isn't possible because time won't allow I'll always phone to discuss the price, what it includes and so on. That way I can gauge whether or not it's worth the cost of sending a written estimate, or of course book an appointment to have the work done. You can confirm the price and date in your letter.

Working out your prices

Success depends on getting your pricing right. Charge too much and you won't get any business. Undercharge and you'll get lots of business that won't make you any money and consequently you'll go bust.

> **When you're asked to quote for a particular job that involves, as most will, more than one job, always put the bulk of your earnings and profit in the main, heavy part of the job.**

Here's an example of what I'm talking about.

Let's imagine for a moment that your prospective client asks you round to have a look at their back garden. When you get there she shows you a large currently overgrown area, which is surrounded by a path and perimeter fencing. She outlines what she wants and this includes:

◆ the entire garden cleared of everything, and everything removed from the site
◆ the area levelled and prepared for turfing
◆ the existing fence replaced.

Obviously, this is a good job if you can get it. So you're keen to give a fair price, and there's nothing wrong with that. But, and here's the but, don't be tempted into charging less for each individual job than you would normally were the job not so large, because you may find that after you've sent your estimate your client only asks you to go ahead with part of the job. This isn't uncommon.

Problems arise when, in your enthusiasm to get the big job, you decide that you'll give a fairly keen price for clearing the main garden and earn your profit on the frills such as the fencing and turfing. Then to your horror your prospective client phones accepting your estimate, but only wants you to clear the main garden. They'll do the fun bit like laying the turf and so on.

> **The most difficult bit of any aspect of gardening is preparing the site. Build sufficient profit into this part of the job, as this may eventually be the only job your client asks you to do.**

I cannot stress the importance of this enough. With some turf suppliers now offering a free laying service, more and more clients now only want the ground prepared for turfing. So make sure you charge enough for the items that you know your client will either not be willing or able to do themselves. *By doing this you can ensure that in the event that only part of your original estimate is accepted, at least you will still earn profit.*

Some other issues

You will need to consider:

◆ Where you're going to physically locate your business.
◆ Whether or not you're going to employ staff.
◆ How you're going to cope with the pressures of running this type of business on a day-to-day basis.

Where are you going to locate your business?

◆ from home
◆ rented premises
◆ friend's or relative's property.

Working from home

By far the best place to base your fledgling business is in your own home. This of course will depend on the amount of space you have available and whether or not you have off-street parking, garage and your own garden.

If you have all these things then great! But with most new properties now coming with postage sized parking, one space per family, and a garden that you would be hard pressed to fit in a 6x4′ greenhouse, you may well find that you're unable to run your business from home. And even if you have the space available, do you really want to clog it up with a van, trailer and whatever else your business will have?

Nothing is surer to bring you into unnecessary conflict with your neighbours and possibly your local council than clogging up the street outside your home with vans and trailers. *You also run considerable risk of having your equipment stolen or vandalised.* Many insurance companies now refuse to insure against theft of equipment that is stored overnight in a vehicle parked on the street.

Renting premises

You may well find that the only option is to find a suitable location to accommodate your business.

Clearly, there's little benefit in renting an office that doesn't have a yard and suitable secure dry storage for your equipment.

Ideally, you should try to find somewhere that:

- is as close to home as possible
- is as cheap as possible
- doesn't involve entering into a long and tedious tenancy agreement
- has secure, dry storage for your tools.

Of course these are ideals and the reality may be somewhat different. But you owe it to yourself to search for the best possible property that you can get. This may mean renting a private garage via your local newspaper. It's a start – and a far more cost-effective way of starting your business than having to enter into some vastly overpriced lease agreement with a shark landlord.

The best way of finding a suitable venue is to scan the **small classified advertisements** in your local papers. *My advice would be that you simply look to rent secure storage space for your equipment and that you base your office at home. Trying to find premises that have both storage space and office space on a limited budget is virtually impossible.*

So if you're unable to locate the tools of your business at home, then you should aim to locate the administration side of your business at home, even if this means locating your business systems on some spare shelf and making do with the kitchen table when available. The savings are still worth it.

Outward appearances of success come at a high price.

Wherever possible you must resist the temptation to spend money. One of the hidden dangers of any business, and certainly this is true of this one, is the tendency to imagine that in order to make a success of things you must first have all the outwards trappings of business success – the office or yard, the telephone answering service, the web site, state-of-the-art gardening tools. Trust me – you don't need any of them. Certainly not to begin with. Remember my motto:

Expand your business from profits, not borrowings.

Are you going to employ staff?

Whether or not you're going to employ staff depends very much on where you see your business going. If you're planning to tackle large jobs then obviously you won't be able to do it without hiring help of some kind.

Beware – becoming an employer brings with it some large, and some would say very onerous responsibilities. Employing a workforce, even one employee, too early in your business can lead to disaster.

My advice is that you steer clear of hiring staff for as long as you possibly can. I would even go as far as to say avoid it completely if you can. There are still ways of employing additional help for those times when you need it, without having to have employees.

Using associates

In my business I use a system of using a number of self-employed associates. This means that I can have a 'workforce' that can be readily called upon whenever the need arises, and dispensed with as soon as the crisis is over. This is the most cost-effective way of running any business.

At the end of the job my associates invoice me for their work, which is always a pre-agreed amount. Usually, they are paid shortly after I have received payment from my client, which means there is no negative impact on my cash flow.

This system has many advantages.

♦ You only pay for labour when you need it.

♦ You don't have to pay sickness pay or holiday pay.

♦ You are not responsible for PAYE and National Insurance.

♦ Often the arrangement is reciprocal – they employ you as a self-employed person when their businesses need help.

I cannot stress the advantages of this arrangement strongly enough. You would do well to find someone who you can call upon on when needed and will work for you on a self-employed basis.

With regard to Employer's Liability Insurance, you will have to cover them under your policy. Even though they will be acting in a self-employed capacity, they will be working under your direction, therefore you're responsible for their insurance.

Coping with the day-to-day pressures of this business

While the rewards from this business are great, so too are the pressures, and how you cope with these will ultimately determine whether or not your business will succeed.

Generally, your time will be spent:

♦ Physically working on the various jobs you have in hand.

♦ In the evenings working out written estimates, returning phone calls and ensuring that your business is on the right track.

Case study – my business

My day begins early – usually 7am when I'm up checking my diary to make sure that:

♦ Everything I need for the day's job is packed in the van.
♦ I have a list of all the people I need to phone that day and that their telephone numbers are included in my daily planner.
♦ Anything I need for the coming few days in the way of materials or stock has been ordered.

The easiest way to ensure that your business runs as smoothly and as stress-free as possible is to ensure that you have a system whereby you can forward-plan.

Here's an example from my diary.

Monday
Work

Hedge trimming and pruning job at Mrs Cassells. I've booked the full day for this work.

To-do – daytime list

I need to make all of these calls during the daytime as they largely involve contacting businesses that will be closed by the time I get home.

1. Order turfing for next week's lawn job – (telephone number).
2. Phone Mr Madden and finalise a date for his pruning job.
3. Book additional help for next Wednesday's turf-laying.
4. Check with builders' suppliers that the paving slabs I ordered last week have arrived and are now available.
5. If they are, then phone Mrs Cottrell and book an appointment to come and lay them.

Evening list

1. Return any calls that I have been unable to make during the day and check the answerphone for new messages.
2. Complete Mr Harper's estimate and phone to discuss it with him. Offer a provisional start date of the first week in June.

In addition to having a daily to-do list, I also have:

- weekly to-do list
- monthly to-do list.

Weekly to-do list

What's included on this list varies depending on the time of the year and proximity to the month end. I include anything that I need to do during the week but that could be done on any day, for example checking my business account online, or devoting time to maintaining and cleaning tools.

Monthly to-do list

This list includes such things as:

- Formulating next month's, or next season's advertising campaign.
- Reviewing past month's performance in terms of both sales achieved and the cost of sales (how much it cost the business to provide a service).
- Paying monthly accounts.
- Looking at new ways of developing the business.
- Filing and dealing with general administration.

As your business develops and expands you must have a system in place where you work from to-do lists. It's vital for you and your business that you know what you have to do in order to keep your business running smoothly, and, more importantly, when you're going to do it.

As I said at the start of the chapter, I really do believe that is the greatest business in the world to run. It's enormous fun. It's relatively profitable and, in terms of satisfaction, nothing will ever beat the feeling you get when you close your client's garden gate for the last time, look back and see that you really have made a difference!

Summary

1. Only purchase items as a part of a pre-planned, phased-in purchasing programme.

2. If you have to borrow money to start your business, only do so if this is going to be a short-term arrangement. Don't tie yourself into costly, long-term bank loans.

3. To begin with run your business with the minimum of equipment and wherever possible avoid buying electric tools. Purchase tools that are capable of independent power sources. If you can't afford a petrol hedge-trimmer use clipping shears.

4. Prepare a workable, achievable business plan for your first 12 months and monitor your progress on a monthly basis.

5. Expand your business from profits and not borrowings.

6. When calculating estimates, remember to detail all the costs associated with the job and allow yourself sufficient hours in which to complete whatever it is that's being asked of you.

7. Where possible don't post your written estimates, try to discuss them either during your initial meeting with your client. If this is not possible, try phoning your client and discussing the job and how much it's likely to cost with them before you send anything in writing.

8. Make sure that you always include an element of profit in everything you do. This is not being greedy, but sensible practice. You need money in your business to cover future essential expenditure such as replacement of your equipment, insurance cover etc.

9. If you're constantly getting all the jobs you've quoted for – then your prices are too low. You should aim for a 70% closure rate. If you can achieve this you're well on the road to success.

10. Make sure that you, your client and your business are adequately insured *before* you start trading. Your home and everything else is at risk if you don't.

11. Planning is the key to success. You must be able to handle a number of projects all at the one time and still ensure that every one of your clients is made to feel special.

12. If you're to make this type of business a success, you must enjoy running it. The general gardening business isn't for everyone and, if it's not for you, there are lots of alternative gardening businesses you can still run.

CHAPTER FIVE

Seasonal Opportunities

This chapter looks at other gardening businesses.

The benefit of spin-offs

Every business has what are often referred to as **'spin-off' opportunities**. This is where you offer additional services that complement your existing business.

How does it work?

In the autumn you will invariably be asked to dig over and prepare the ground for next year's planting. In most cases it would be beneficial if you enhance the soil with some quality compost, and depending on the quantity of perennial weeds apparent in the soil, it may be necessary to include in the job some weed eradication. For example, covering the prepared ground with black polyethylene to prevent further weed growth.

So in addition to digging over the soil in preparation for the winter frosts, you could also offer your client:

- quality compost
- weed preventative membrane
- if the ground is particularly hard, you could also include a dressing of sharp sand to enhance drainage.

Thus what started out as a simple digging over job can include the sale of sand, compost and weed membrane all of which, you should have no difficulty obtaining at trade prices, allowing you sufficient mark-up for profit.

> The important thing is that you look for spin-off opportunity in everything you do. This way you can maximise your sales on every job, making even the most dismal of tasks profitable and perhaps even enjoyable.

Clients will appreciate what you're doing

If you have any reservations about introducing spin-offs into your business and feel that it's all a bit too pushy, then let me set your mind at ease. Many, if not all, of your clients will not be gardeners. This is why they will be employing you. What better way to help your client than suggesting what they need and offering to provide it? Nothing will frustrate your clients more than telling them when you've finished digging over their garden that the ground could do with having compost dug through it, or a dressing of sand applied to improve drainage.

> Spin-offs are just as important to your client as they are to your business. Try to include an extra in every job you do, even if it's only a bag of mushroom compost.

Now is the time to review the service/s you are proposing to offer and see what extras you can include.

You can specialise

Gardening by its sheer diversity offers so much in terms of flexibility that you can make any one of the businesses that follow fit comfortably into a few hours or days a week, whatever is compatible with your lifestyle. You don't have to offer a general gardening service.

Here are some of the services that you can offer:

◆ lawn-cutting service
◆ build it and fix-it service
◆ mobile plant nursery
◆ gardening coaching service.

Lawn-cutting service

By far the most price sensitive and cut-throat of all the gardening businesses, lawn-cutting can be profitable and enjoyable, the main drawback being its seasonal nature. Some of the operators I know work every daylight hour available during the lawn cutting season and spend their winters holidaying and enjoying themselves. If you're reading this book in the winter, then this lifestyle has its appeal.

The spin-off factor

There are a number of additional services that you can offer to complement your main business and make sure that you have enough work to see you through the dormant period when lawns are not growing:

- aeration
- scarification
- turf laying
- repairing worn or damaged areas
- weeding.

There's no reason for your business to be quiet just because the lawns are not growing.

Pricing

Lawn-cutting is a volume business. Prices tend to be keen, with larger operators taking over complete neighbourhoods. They arrive with a fleet of lawn mowers and an operator for each mower. Lawns are cut in double quick time, cuttings are thrown into high-sided trailers, or wheelie bins carried in the back of the van. Their service resembles that of a refuse collection in terms of speed and quality. The name of the game is to cut as many lawns as quickly as possible and move on. There's little time for brushing up afterwards, although many do have someone brushing up as they go. However, they too are under the clock and with so little time and so much grass they struggle to do the job efficiently. What amazes me is that people are willing to pay for what is generally a poor service. Of course there are those who do a wonderful job and leave everywhere looking tidy and free from clippings. Some even cut the lawn edges. But this is rare.

Setting up a lawn-cutting operation

Starting a large operation like the one above is difficult. It requires a lot in the way of capital to purchase the vehicle, trailer and lawn mowers necessary to do the job. Most areas will already have these businesses so it can be difficult for a newcomer to break in. *If you really want to go down this route then you could consider purchasing an existing business complete with clients and equipment.* Of course you'll need to check carefully to see what you're buying, but assuming that what you're being offered has at least three years' trading figures (don't consider anything else), which show a good profit, then and only then investigate further. Once you are satisfied have an accountant look over the books. Bona fide sellers will expect this. If they start shrugging and taking offence because you've told them your accountant will need to see their books, walk away.

This applies to any existing business that you may be looking to buy. Make sure that you know what's been offered in terms of both return on your investment and the business's reputation.

My own opinion is that you are far better starting your own lawn-cutting service than buying an existing one. By starting afresh you can avoid much of the 'baggage' that undoubtedly will come with an established business.

There's always room for a quality, more personal lawn-cutting service.

Despite the relative success and saturation of the big boys, there is lots of room for a professional lawn-cutting service. Your service should include the following:

♦ Quality, professional cut using a reliable, well-maintained mower that is suitable for the lawn you are cutting.

♦ Keeping the edges razor sharp with an edging tool or shears.

♦ Brushing up after you have finished.

♦ Never filling your fuel tank on your client's property. Or if you must, making sure that you put sit your mower on some protective covering to avoid damage to patios, lawns and driveways caused by fuel and oil spillages.

♦ Tailoring your service to suit individual clients' needs.

♦ Where possible avoiding cutting lawns in inclement weather.

If you offer more than the volume operators by way of quality, then you don't have to sell on price. This is true of all gardening businesses. You should never compete on price alone.

There will always be somebody who'll do it cheaper.

What you do need to make sure is that your service offers more in the way of benefits than the larger operators. So when your potential client says 'How much? Lawn-Cutting Cowboys are doing it for half that!' You can explain that while Lawn-Cutting Cowboys are cheaper, they do not include in their service edging and brushing up everywhere once they've finished, which means that the client is left to do it themselves. This is the benefit of hiring you.

You can also incorporate lawn-cutting into your existing business. This type of business is ideal to include with your gardening round. If you offer a weekly lawn-cutting service and undertake to maintain the client's garden at the same time, then you really will be in demand.

Tools of the trade

You must invest in a mower that is capable of working all day, every day. You'll find these at specialised garden shops catering for the trade. Check your *Yellow Pages*. Dealers usually sell or hire a wide range of gardening equipment including chainsaws, strimmers etc. Unless you're planning to cut only a few lawns a week, you would be well advised to invest in a commercial mower. Prices start at around £400. They're not cheap, but they are capable of working long hours without overheating and becoming problematic. Mowers you find at DIY stores are generally only suitable for domestic work. Guarantees are invalidated if you use them for anything other than mowing your own lawn.

Or use your client's mower.

The alternative to purchasing your own mower is to use your clients', provide of course they have one. There are many keen gardeners who have grown too old to mow their own lawn and will be only too happy to have a professional cut it for them.

So you could offer a service whereby you provide the labour and your client provides the mower. Nothing wrong with this and it'll save you having to invest in, and service, your own mower.

Potential earnings

Your earnings will depend on how many lawns you cut and at what price. If you want to make a full-time, profitable business from lawn cutting, my advice is that you aim to cut fewer lawns but charge more because of the quality of your workmanship.

Don't underestimate what's involved. Even a self-propelled mower becomes hard work when you're doing it all day. There's a lot of bending down and emptying grass boxes as well as moving heavy garden furniture such as tables and chairs away from the lawn prior to cutting, and putting them back once you've finished. Don't underestimate the work involved. This business involves far more than pushing a mower around.

When quoting for a job you will need to consider:

- The size and area of the lawn to be cut.

- Whether or not you will be able to cut it using your mower, or the layout is such that you will have to use a strimmer for those tight corners.

- Does your contract include removing the grass clippings? If so, remember to include enough to cover tipping charges.

- How much garden furniture will you have to move from the lawn before you cut it?

- Dog fouling – if your client has a dog who is responsible for clearing away the dog mess prior to the cutting? If it's you, make sure you charge enough. From personal experience, I can tell you this can be very time-consuming, particularly if your client is elderly and unable to do it for themselves. My experience was that before I could begin cutting, I'd have to clear away a week's worth of dog mess. Invariably this took longer than actually cutting the lawn.

When cutting the lawns you should always wear:

- protective ear muffs
- heavy-duty gardening gloves
- steel capped boots
- protective eye glasses when using strimmers and the like.

Build it and fix-it service

Most gardens have structures that will need erecting or repairing. Whether it's a tired but much loved greenhouse in need of some weatherproofing or a new roof for a summerhouse, there is always opportunity for a skilled handyman.

> **If you're a skilled DIYer or a retired professional carpenter,**
> **then there is a ready-made market for your skills.**

Increasingly, hard structures are now coming flat-packed, which can cause headaches. If you're in any doubt, stand near to the customer services counter of any large DIY store on a Saturday and Sunday and you'll see what I mean.

Not everyone is capable of erecting a greenhouse. There's no shame in that. However, people don't like to admit to it. The same goes for garden sheds, fencing and benches. *The key to offering a build-it service is that you don't make yourself look clever and your client foolish.*

Be careful how you market this service. Your sales literature needs to highlight the benefits of having someone else erect their greenhouse or shed while they get on with enjoying their garden and the long summer days.

> **Base any sales campaign, literature, advertisement or card on the basis of selling the benefits of**
> **employing your experience, rather than 'If you can't erect your shed, I'll do it for you', approach.**

An all-year-round business

Spend your summers building the latest in gardening gismos and the winter repairing them!

There will always be a need for a skilled professional to come and repair a leaking greenhouse, re-erect or replace a wind-torn fence panel. This really is an excellent year-round business to run for those who love DIYing. You can either run this as a business in itself, or add it as an additional service to a gardening round or other business.

Operating costs

The costs involved in starting such a business are relatively low, assuming that you already have many of the tools. Other than those, there are the following costs to consider:

◆ insurance
◆ advertising
◆ cost of providing and running a vehicle

- your time
- tax.

This is an ideal way for those planning to run a gardening round to bridge that seasonal gap between October and March, ensuring that you keep a steady flow of cash coming into your business.

> My own experience is that during those awful months when all hell breaks loose with the weather our phone never stops with requests for assistance with fencing, walls, greenhouses, sheds and just about everything else.

Potential earnings

Unlike the gardening round, earnings are not as easily predicted. Initially your earnings may be low to non-existent while you spend time establishing your business and getting your name known. The more pro-active and imaginative you are with your sales strategy, the quicker your business will take off.

The key to success with this business is a well thought-out sales strategy.

It's a good idea to approach every business, no matter how large, in your area that sells greenhouses, sheds and the like. Ask them if will they allow you to display a leaflet advertising your assembly services. Stress to them that it's in their interests as it means their customers can not only buy the product, but not have to worry about assembling it. Often the larger DIY chains have already got a local company which assembles on their behalf. However, they may not always be available so it's worth leaving your card. *A press release to your local newspaper is also a great way of getting some free publicity and generating interest.* Try to make a story out of your business. Editors don't print ads, they sell them.

Some well-placed advertisements outlining your emergency repair service will yield dividends. The main cost of providing this service is the vehicle. You don't necessarily need a van, although if you have one it is certainly very useful. Alternatively, you could consider using a small trailer. You will also have to allow in your costings a budget for ongoing advertising. Future clients may see your advertisement and think what a good idea, but have no need for your service at that time, so it's important to agree the best rates possible and keep your ad running.

Mobile plant nursery

If you enjoy growing plants this is an ideal way to turn a hobby into a business.

Provided you have space available in your garden to keep your plants, then this business can be run successfully from home without having to rent any property. It involves you:

- either growing the plants from seeds, or purchasing 'plug plants' and bringing them on

- then selling your plants at car boot fairs, exhibitions, shows, markets etc.

It's a relatively straightforward business to run and can be very profitable. But if your plan is to run this business on a large scale, then the best way to approach it is to find the nearest plant wholesalers to you and request a copy of their catalogue. It's unlikely that you will have either the time or the space to grow and propagate sufficient quantities to make it viable other than as a part-time business.

Wholesalers will do all the initial hard work for you and can supply you in sufficient quantities to ensure you can make a profit. Most wholesalers insist on a minimum order, usually £100 plus VAT, plus carriage.

Getting started

The time of year you launch your business will determine what range of plants you offer. Prior to doing anything you will need to:

- Carry out some initial market research to identify who your customers are likely to be, who your competitors are and where best you can retail your plants.

- Detail all the costs of bringing your product to the market place. Through your initial market research you should get an idea of how much you can realistically expect to charge per plant.

- Work out a profit and loss forecast to see if what you're proposing to sell will cover the costs of buying the plants wholesale, your labour costs, any additional costs – for example packaging and compost – and last but most importantly, an element of profit.

If you enjoy meeting people and have the confidence to sell your plants to all types of people, in all types of situations, then this is a great business to run. You don't need high-street premises, which greatly reduces your outgoings and makes it more viable.

There are a number of things that you must do to ensure your business is both successful and profitable:

◆ Your plants and shrubs must be in top condition.

◆ Don't underestimate the time and labour involved in getting your plants in a saleable condition.

◆ Don't under-price your produce just because you are selling from the 'boot of your car'. Experienced gardeners with an eye for quality will recognise quality when they see it.

◆ As well as offering favourites, try to offer plants that aren't too easy to get elsewhere. For example, good selections of quality culinary and aromatic herbs make great sellers.

◆ Try to find unusual places to sell your plants. For example, events where you wouldn't normally expect to find plants – boat jumbles (boaters tend to be keen gardeners), craft fairs, computer shows and the like. When choosing venues remember that your customers may not be gardeners themselves. Plants and shrubs make excellent, relatively cheap gifts.

Striking the right balance between what to buy and in what quantities can be difficult in the early days. This takes time. *Don't expect overnight success with this venture. But persevere. There is always a market for quality plants and shrubs.*

Catalogue selling

Another way of successfully selling stock is to publish a catalogue. It needn't be anything fancy. If you're a whiz at desktop publishing then you can create your own on your PC. Alternatively recruit a friend to do it and pay them from stock.

Distribute your catalogue to all the local businesses in your area that have more than ten employees. Leave them with an order form and an envelope for the money. Arrange to call back the following week on a pre-arranged date, when you can collect your catalogue and deliver any orders from the stock you carry around in the boot of your car or van.

This is a great way of selling stock. Book publishers have been doing it successfully for years. Make sure that when you do get orders you leave another catalogue together with an order form.

Perfect your salesmanship

Running this business calls for a bit of upfront sales ability. Nothing pushy is needed, just enough confidence to walk through the door, introduce yourself, tell whoever it is you speak to (receptionists are often the best as they know everyone in the company and often wield more influence than the managing director!) that you're offering quality plants and shrubs delivered directly to their office.

On your first visit, and as often as you like thereafter, leave a free sample with whoever had time to speak to you. *Develop and maintain your contacts.* Look after the person who distributes and collects your cash and they will look after you.

Don't be afraid of rejection

If you get a negative reaction don't take it personally, simply thank whoever you spoke to, even if they're as rude as hell to you, and leave.

> **With this business your ability to sell is just as important as your ability to care for and nurture your plants.**

Gardening coaching service

Running your own garden coaching service can be a useful way of generating extra income during the summer months. It is ideal for anyone looking for an extra income and where you don't have to do all the heavy work associated with many of the other gardening businesses we've looked at.

To run your own gardening coaching company you will need to:

- be a confident public speaker who enjoys meeting people
- be an experienced, well-read gardener

- have lots of patience
- not be flustered or put off by difficult people.

Success depends not just on your gardening experience, but your ability to get on with people and make them feel comfortable in your presence. Some of your clients may already have good basic gardening skills, while others won't know an annual from a perennial.

Being a gardening coach can be great fun, provided you have sufficient knowledge, and equally important are confidence and patience in dealing with all sorts of people.

Getting started

To get your business off the ground, you will need to:

- identify your skills
- carry out initial market research – who is your service primarily aimed at?
- work out a pricing structure
- advertise your service.

Your skills

The more knowledge you have the better. Write down all the gardening skills you have. Then identify those that you feel most confident with. If your knowledge and expertise is the creating and maintaining of lawn care, then offer a service where you will teach others how to create a new lawn, or restore an existing one. Or if you're an all-round expert then offer an all-round coaching service.

Market research

Gardening coaching is something that has yet to take off in this country. But that doesn't mean that there isn't a market out there waiting for your services. It wasn't long ago that personal fitness coaches were unheard of. This is now a thriving industry. *So be brave and be a trend setter – get coaching!*

Your potential clients

Obviously much of your business is going to come from people who have little or no gardening experience, but want to learn. They'll fall into two categories:

- Those who want to learn more about how to care for a garden they already have.

- Those who want to create a new garden and need advice and help with planning, creating and caring for it.

The property pages of your local newspaper can be a good place to get a feel for what's going on in your area, where the new houses are being built and how many purchasers are first-time buyers.

Working out a pricing structure

With this business, you're selling your knowledge and experience. The people who hire you as their coach will generally be those who wish to garden for themselves, but lack either the confidence or ability.

My advice is that you adopt a similar strategy in relation to pricing your service as would a personal trainer. To do this, you will first need to:

1. Arrange an initial meeting with your client or clients (you'll find this service popular amongst couples) to discuss their requirements.

2. From this work out a coaching programme. This could involve you spending anything from one day to a whole week at their garden working through their requirements.

More often than not, you'll be asked to help out in relation to an existing garden. If this is the case, then you should include a garden maintenance plan in your coaching programme.

Once you've identified your clients' coaching needs, which could be anything from a day spent advising and working through a propagating regime to one day every month working through the garden's seasonal requirements, you will be in a position to arrive at a price.

> **There's no hard and fast rule for how much you should charge.**
> **It's a matter for you to determine how much your time is worth.**

But don't underestimate the work involved in coaching and make sure that you charge enough from the outset to make the work both fun and profitable for yourself.

When calculating your fees make sure you include sufficient to cover the following:

- The time you spent actually coaching.

- Your administration time in preparing a written coaching programme and maintenance notes.

- Stationery costs, postage etc.

- Your research time. Even with vast amounts of experience, coaching is an exercise where you will have to carry out some research. Make sure you include this in your costings.

For those with sufficient experience and confidence in their ability, this really is a super business to run. It doesn't involve hours of back-breaking slog and can, if you get your pricing right, be profitable.

Always something to do in the garden

When deciding on what gardening business to run, don't be afraid to explore new ideas and offer innovative services.

Don't ignore the small jobs – they lead to the bigger ones

One of jobs that I'm forever being asked to do is to plant up pots and tubs with seasonal bedding at the start of the season, then return in the autumn to clear the pots out and re-plant with seasonal bulbs. The pots owners are keen gardeners themselves, who for a variety of reasons, often old age and failing health, cannot do it themselves.

> Planting the tubs and containers is great fun and by doing it I've got to know some very lovely people. I've also learnt a lot, as these clients have spent a lifetime devoted to what they love doing the most – gardening.

Small is not just beautiful – it can also be very profitable.

Whatever business you run, don't turn away the small jobs, the ones that may appear on the face of it to require little more than an hour or so of your time. For it is from these types of jobs that you will get some excellent referral work. In turn this means that your business matures, you will have to spend less on advertising, which results in less expenditure.

> Your aim should always be to reduce the amount you spend on advertising. Gardening is a referral business. Build your reputation and pretty soon your clients will come knocking on your door. If they don't then you need to ask yourself why.

Summary

- Spin-offs are what make a good business great. Not only will they provide an additional income stream for your business, but also greatly enhance the service you're already providing.

- Don't be afraid to specialise. Treat every aspect of gardening as a separate entity. For example, hedge-trimming is a business in itself, in the same way lawn-cutting is. Rose care is also a specialised area. If you're particularly good at something then concentrate on this and become an expert in that field.

- Beware of entering into any price-cutting war. Without proper market research you run the risk of inadvertently undercutting your competitors as well as damaging the market. Sell on the basis of the quality of your service, not on price.

- Don't turn the small jobs down. People like to try before they buy and often will ask you to do something relatively small and simple before deciding to get you to tackle all the things on their list.

CHAPTER SIX

Launching Your Business

This chapter looks at sowing the seeds of success.

Preparing for growth

Some further ground work

Prior to starting your business you will need to be clear on two very important issues namely, identifying your:

- potential clients
- competitors.

By now you should have a fairly good idea of the type of services you are going to offer. You should also have a written draft of your business plan completed prior to starting. If in the future you wish to deviate from this initial plan, that's fine. *Your plan will provide an important framework for you to start your business with. See it as a map guiding you through your first few days, weeks and months.* There is nothing wrong with re-writing it as you go along. What's important at this stage is that you have considered and fully investigated the following:

- Details of the services you are proposing to offer.
- Who these services are targeted at.
- How much you're planning to charge.
- How this compares with current market prices in your area.
- Knowledge of your competitors and reasons clients would choose you as opposed to them.
- An initial profit and loss forecast to cover your first six months of trading. Hopefully you'll go as far as working out one for your first year.

Potential clients

Initially it can be very difficult to identify who your clients are likely to be. Anyone with a garden, no matter how small, is a potential client. The key to successfully growing your business is that you gain referrals from your first clients. Not only will this save you future advertising costs, but you will also benefit from quickly establishing your reputation. This is why you must carefully research your initial pricing structure.

If you're too cheap you'll end up with a flood of unprofitable business, which will eventually lead to your demise. Too expensive and you won't get any work.

> **Prior to starting you must research the rates that your competitors are currently charging. This is something you cannot leave to trial and error.**

Researching the going rates

The nature of gardening businesses means that there is no high street shop for you to pop into and browse in order to glean what your competitors are charging. Occasionally you may find that gardeners advertise their hourly rates in newsagents' windows or at the end of their published ads. If you come across such advertisements, you should never take the rates quoted as indicative of local prices. By all means include them in your research but don't solely rely on them.

Research methods. There are many ways of researching what your competitors are charging, but by far the simplest way is to simply phone them up and ask for a quote.

General gardening

If you're planning to run a general gardening business, one where you tackle a wide variety of work, then phone up a number of companies and ask them for a rough idea of how much it would cost to have a specific job done, for example trim a hedge. If, as I suspect many will, they tell you that they can only provide an estimate if they come and see what needs to be done, you could either arrange to have them visit a friend's garden, or press them for a rough idea of charges by giving them the hedge's measurements etc.

What will become apparent as you work your way through your competitors is that many are in fact not your competitors at all. Some of the businesses you phone will no longer be trading. Or if they are, will no longer be undertaking the type of work that you'll be doing. This is particularly true of businesses that advertise in annual directories such as the *Yellow Pages* and *Thompson Directories*.

Then there will be those you phone who will tell you they are now fully booked for the next few months and invite you to try someone else. Others will be so rude and unhelpful and suspicious of your calling them that under no circumstances would you have them anywhere near your property let alone working in your prized garden.

Your findings

Despite starting out with what may appear to be a fairly comprehensive list of local gardening companies you will soon narrow this down to a small group of competitors, those that:

◆ Are pleasant, and approachable when you phone them.
◆ Appear professional and knowledgeable.
◆ Return your call on the same day or first thing the following morning.
◆ Are upfront with their prices.

These are the businesses that you will be competing against so it is important that your prices are in line with this group.

Don't fall into the trap of undercutting your competitors to get the business.

Initially, you may be tempted to undercut your competitors as a way of introducing your business to the market place. *Don't*. It's a fool's game, which will only lead to problems.

At the beginning of every season a whole new batch of gardening companies enters my area, people like myself who for a variety of reasons have decided to set up their own business. Without fail a proportion of these operators try to win business by lowering their prices. Consequently these enterprises rarely if at all survive beyond their first season. As soon as they realise just how much hard work is involved and how inadequate their fees are, they soon come to the conclusion that it's far better being an employee than self-employed.

The vast majority of gardening outfits are one-man bands and there is nothing wrong with this. In my opinion this is the best way to operate, at least in the early days when learning how to run your business. *So if you're tempted to undercut the going rates remember that there is a physical limit to how much work each of your competitors can undertake.* There are only so many hedges, lawns, trees that any one person can cut in one day. Don't despair if you see a page full of gardening service adverts in your local papers. It doesn't take long for them all to become fully booked, particularly during spring and autumn.

Don't compare your prices with non-professionals'

Your research will demonstrate that despite the amount of gardeners offering their services, few operate in a professional way. Many 'gardeners' offer all sorts of additional services including rubbish clearance, window cleaning, painting and decorating, pet sitting to name a few. Would you be confident entrusting your prized rose collection to someone who is an all-round handyman? No, of course you wouldn't. These are the gardeners who qualify their advertisements with the cheery 'we'll beat any price' slogan. The reason they can do this is they quite literally hack their way through gardening. I've seen so many once beautiful shrubs destroyed by these merchants and so many plants killed off by improper and inappropriate use of weed killers and the like.

> There's nothing cheap and cheerful about a dead hedge, or roses that have been hacked to death. Never be afraid to charge for professional gardening. Knowledge, expertise and experience comes at a price. Don't undersell your service.

When clients employ a gardener their decision about whom to use will not be based on price alone. There are lots of factors, the main ones being:

- ability to do the job
- professionalism
- reputation
- availability.

Availability is another reason why you should never discount your prices or charge anything below market rates.

Were someone to ask me to do some work for them I would have to tell them that the soonest I could do it would be at least the following month. My diary is always that full. While most of my clients will wait, there are some who need the job done immediately.

Thus they may well phone you. So if when you give them a price you deliberately undercut my rates in the hope that you will get the business, you will in fact be undercutting yourself as opposed to me. See the difference?

This is a costly mistake for you to make because in my experience, no matter what the price, people will always expect you to do a first class job, which is only normal. You couldn't imagine someone phoning you up and asking you to come over and hack their roses to death for £5 an hour, could you? People will expect, as they should, that you will provide an excellent service. That's why they have phoned you as opposed to the advertisement that stated they'd beat any price.

Your availability to do the job is often more important to people than what you charge them.

The butcher's tale

A woman walks into a butcher's shop and asks for six lamb chops. While the butcher is preparing and trimming the meat she notices the price. 'Gosh,' she says, 'I didn't think they'd be that expensive.' The butcher stops what he's doing and looks at her. 'Sorry, Madam,' he says, 'do you still want them?'

'Well, the shop across the road is selling six chops for £2.50. But you're selling them for £3.00.'

'So why don't you buy them there?' the butcher asks.

'Because they haven't got any.'

The butcher smiles. 'Madam, if I hadn't got any I'd sell them to you for £1.50 for six.'

This is an old story and one that's used often by sales trainers. But there's a good lesson there. Beware of competing on price alone. You're not selling a product. You're selling a service. Let all the other companies fill their diaries with unprofitable work. Sooner than you think you'll find yourself in demand!

When meeting clients for the first time always bring your diary with you. I cannot stress this enough. The best way to close the sale is to give a price there and then, open your diary and suggest a date. 'Okay Mrs Marsh, to cut the entire hedge, remove the clippings, sweep up afterwards will cost £35.' Then you open your diary and suggest a date sometime in advance. Not tomorrow. You don't want to appear desperate. 'I could do it for you, let's see how about next Thursday morning at 9am?'

This is the simplest way of closing any sale. If, and this is a big if, Mrs Marsh says something like: 'That's very expensive. My neighbour had theirs cut for £15 and it was larger than mine,' resist the temptation to look across the road at the hedge, shake your head and say, 'But I'll do it better.'

No. Even if it looks like whoever cut it was drunk when they did it, don't knock their work. Simply say that for you to do Mrs Marsh's hedge it will cost £35. Be prepared to walk away. *There are other clients and plenty more opportunities. But if you discount your prices now you'll have the whole street wanting you to cut their hedges for £15 or whatever you finally agree on, and soon you'll be rushed off your feet and earning nothing.*

The real competition

If your proposed business will involve offering gardening makeovers and the like, then the competition is not just other landscaping companies quoting for the business.

The decision to spend £5,000 on having a garden makeover is something that most homeowners will give considerable thought to. And unless you're very fortunate and your potential clients have oodles of money then you will find yourself competing against foreign holidays, new cars, washing machines, home furnishings and the like.

If makeovers and building new gardens are to form a core part of your business then you will need to be confident in your sales ability. Convincing your client that a new garden is better than two weeks in some far-flung exotic place isn't too difficult provided you remember the golden rule of selling, which is:

People buy benefits not features.

A complete garden makeover might have the following features:

- re-designed lawn area
- better use of space
- all year-round colour
- low maintenance garden.

But the benefits are:

◆ Landscaped gardens increase the value of the property.

◆ The garden will be somewhere you can enjoy all-year round and not just for two weeks.

◆ By having a low maintenance garden you can either enjoy more free time by having less gardening work to do, or reduce the amount you spend on garden maintenance.

Sell the benefits, not the features: 'By creating a new, low maintenance garden Mrs Smith, you'll have far more time available to play your golf and you won't feel as tired.'

My biggest competitor

I've come to the conclusion that my biggest competitor is the travel agent. Even in the aftermath of the tragic events of 11 September 2001, I lost considerable business when the airlines began to offer discounted holidays to tempt people back to travelling. A number of my clients who had previously booked me to re-design their gardens phoned to cancel as they were now planning an extended winter vacation and the garden could wait until the following year.

There's not much you can do when this happens. It's a difficult thing to convince someone that they'll be far happier with their newly laid turf than they will topping up their winter tan on some sun drenched shore.

I say difficult, but not impossible. For it didn't stop me re-contacting them in the spring, when their tans were fading and they were getting round to thinking about how they'd spent the rest of the year looking at their overgrown garden.

Remember you're running a business. To be successful you must be prepared to sell and seek out those opportunities that make an already good business great.

Some excellent sources for researching both your potential clients and competitors in your area are:

- local newspaper

- council publications – newspapers, newsletters etc

- the shops in your high street, town centre, village etc – upmarket or bargain basement?

- magazine and paper racks in your local newsagents – what are people reading – *Homes and Gardens*, or *Crime Weekly*?

- libraries

- brochures for adult education classes.

Ongoing research

It's a good idea to have an ongoing market research strategy. This is particularly important after you complete your first few months of trading, and indeed I would recommend that you do it on a regular basis throughout the year. It's a very useful way of ensuring that your business is in line with your competitors and keeping abreast of current developments.

The competition

I have two main competitors – two local gardening companies who I know do a splendid job and are professional in every way. Rather than see them as a threat, I like to see them as allies. I don't begrudge them their success and whenever I bump into them out and about I always stop and have a chat with them. We all enjoy a healthy relationship. If there's something I can't do, if I'm unavailable or on holiday, and my client is desperate, I'll gladly recommend my two competitors. When I've mentioned this to people in the past they've thought I've been foolish, arguing that by recommending the competition, especially the good ones, I lose my clients for good. This hasn't happened. In fact the opposite is true, I have strengthened my relationship with them as they have come to trust me even more. I also ensure that if I am to 'lose' any business at least I'm happy in the knowledge that the professional will get it as opposed to the cheap hacker. The referral system works two ways as there are often times when my competitors refer clients to me.

Make friends with the competition. It'll pay dividends.

Creating the right image

Before you start you need to give some thought to your image, and how prospective customers are likely to see you.

Put simply – you are your business's shop window.

Few would disagree that creating a positive business image is vital to success. Many people see a successful business as one with lots of employees, fancy offices, brochures, shiny vehicles and large glossy advertisements. The more you have, the more successful you must be, right?

It's ironic that large businesses spend oodles of money employing all sorts of image consultants and advertising agencies to make them look like a small, family run, caring enterprise, while small businesses that offer so much in the way of personal service, putting pride before profit, spend much time and energy trying to make their operations appear larger than they actually are in the mistaken belief that this will impress people. Odd, don't you think?

Small is beautiful

Gardening is one business where clients will appreciate a personal service. Someone who:

◆ is competent and capable

◆ turns up when they say they will, or phones if they can't

◆ charges a fair price for what they do.

This is the business where small really is beautiful, where the one-man band really is the orchestra. When people phone your business they're not going to have to select from a list of options that make them wish they'd never called. They're not going to have to listen to some awful, recurring music and then, when eventually they get through, be asked a whole string of personal questions.

> Your clients are your future. You won't need to know who their mother was or what are the last two digits from their passwords, because everyone who phones you will be made to feel as if they are your only client. This is the key to both recruiting and retaining your clientele. Make them feel that they are special.

You must be professional in all your dealings with callers even if they're trying to sell you something.

Case study

A short time after I had my dedicated business line installed, I began to be plagued by all sorts of companies trying to sell me things I didn't want. Some of the businesses go to enormous lengths to disguise that they're trying to sell you anything. One day a lady phoned asking me whether or not I took credit cards. When I told her I didn't, she asked why. Trying not to show my increasing irritation, I told her we only took cash or cheques and enquired what it was she wanted me to do for her. As I suspected, she was trying to sell me the latest credit card processing gismo. I had to listen to a painful reading from her pre-prepared script, which outlined all the reasons why I should invest in such a thing, but she never once asked me whether or not my business had a bank account.

Trying to stop her was like trying to eradicate a nasty dose of ground elder – virtually impossible. When I finally managed to tell her that I did not want whatever it was that she was selling, she replied by slamming the phone down.

Interruptions like these are commonplace when running your own business. Get used to it, people will call you all the time trying to sell you something.

Until that lady's call, I had never had someone ask me whether we took credit cards. Two days later the phone rang again.

'Hello, do you take credit cards?'

Cautiously and resisting the urge to bite her head off, I told her we didn't.

'Oh not to worry. Do you take cheques?'

Still convinced this was another selling tactic, I told her rather abruptly that we did.

'Great,' she replied. 'I need a lot of work done in my garden and everyone I've phoned so far is insisting on cash only.'

Treat all callers with respect

Whoever phones, whether it's someone trying to sell you something, a wrong number, or hopefully a prospective client, you won't really know until you speak with them. *My advice is to always answer the phone as if it were an important client.* Be courteous, be professional and don't pre-judge the caller even if someone is trying to flog you something that you don't like. You don't know – it may just be to your advantage to be nice to them. And anyway you'll feel better afterwards. Getting annoyed with telephone sales people will achieve nothing.

> One day a local magazine phoned to offer me a special deal on an advertisement in their publication. At the time I was interested. So I had a long discussion with the sales person outlining what my business would do and what I would want included in my ad. The call ended amicably enough with my agreeing to think about it. No heavy sales pressure. I'd call her if I were interested. Next morning the phone rang just as I was having my breakfast. It was someone from the magazine. A different person to the one I had spoken to the previous evening. Somehow I managed to resist the temptation of biting her head for hassling me to buy their advertising space, which was just as well. This person had read their colleague's draft advertisement and was delighted to discover a gardening company who, in her words, she could trust. I visited her garden a few days later, quoted, agreed a price and carried out the job to her satisfaction, and I've also had referral business from both her and her colleagues at the magazine.

Whether you like it or not, you're in business 24 hours a day, seven days a week.

It's vital to maintain a professional image wherever you are, especially when you're not working.

> I've bumped into clients at all sorts of places, most popular being the supermarket. If they look as if they want to have a chat, I'll always make some time for them even if it's only a quick 'how's your garden going?'.

Be aware that, wherever you are from now on, people will see you as the gardener, or the landscaper or the person who comes and cuts our lawn. Your clients, past, future and potential, may be watching you so your professional image should be maintained at all times not just when you're working.

> **Even when your diary is full of work and you have a queue of clients waiting for you to come and help them, you must maintain your professionalism.**

Case study – David the gardener

David had been a gardener with the local authority for most of his working life, during which he accumulated a wealth of gardening knowledge, but as soon as he retired he became bored. Unhappy with spending his retirement at home, he decided to offer his services as a gardener and began by putting a few cards up in the local newsagents' windows.

It wasn't long before he had built up his intended three-day-a-week gardening round. The other days were then free for him to indulge in his beloved fishing and spending time chatting with the tourists in the local pubs. It would appear that David is running a successful business. Certainly the first time I spoke to him he told me that he had no end of people approaching him asking for his help.

There were problems though. His price was too cheap at £5 an hour, but he appeared happy with it putting in extra hours if he needed more money. However, the biggest problem with David's business, and one that he failed to see himself, was that he was unreliable. He turned up when he felt like it. His customers never knew when they'd see him again, if ever. And if the weather was particularly good, he'd drop everything and take off fishing. His attitude was that he was retired. Gardening to him was an additional source of income, nothing else.

David failed to see the situation from his customers' perspective. His attitude was that he was working for himself and not them, they were lucky to have someone with his knowledge and experience working in their gardens, and he only charged them a fiver an hour. He hated being tied down. All his working life he had to be somewhere at a given time. This was the part he hated about work. Not the gardening, but turning up in some lousy depot every morning at a given time to be taken to one of the council's municipal gardens, where he'd work until the truck came to take him somewhere else. Now that he's retired, he isn't going back to routine for anyone.

Recently a number of David's clients approached me asking for my help with their gardens. They had grown tired of the way he treated them. When I asked them why they'd suffered him for as long as they had, without exception they all said because there was no one else available. None of them minded having to pay a far higher price to have their gardens looked after. Overnight David became redundant. A victim of his own arrogance.

Never lose sight of the importance of looking after your clients. Sometimes it's all too easy put their needs second to your own. If you do this then at some point you will lose them.
You have been warned.

Creating the right image

The way David had worked his business ensured that at some time his clients would go elsewhere. It was only a matter of time before another gardener entered the market. People will only suffer the sort of service that he became renowned for a short time. They expect, and deserve, a professional, reliable service from their gardener.

While larger operators with their expensive, glossy brochures, tools and high-powered vehicles may appear to have an advantage over your proposed small enterprise this is not always the case. They cannot compete with you when it comes to offering a personal service. So don't ever undersell yourself because you believe yourself to be small and insignificant. *In my experience homeowners prefer dealing with smaller businesses. When it comes to gardens, bigger isn't always better.*

Code of practice

Here are some of the things that I do, or insist on, to ensure that my working day runs that bit smoother:

- Before parking on my client's driveway, I always ask their permission.

- We bring our own refreshments and never expect nor encourage our clients to have their kettle permanently on the boil for us. If offered a cup of tea or coffee, then great.

- Smoking is not allowed while working in a client's garden.

- Neither is the use of mobile phones, personal radios etc. The only exception is my business phone, which is set to vibrate as opposed to ring.

- If the job involves generating any amount of debris on pathways or driveways, where possible we will always lay covers on them. If this is not feasible we'll ensure they are kept clean and in the same condition as when we first arrived.

◆ Tools are not left lying around all over the place inviting accidents and causing inconvenience.

◆ If what we're doing is going to generate noise, for example using a chainsaw, then we inform our client prior to starting.

◆ We treat our client's property as we would wish our own to be treated.

◆ We dress professionally. This means no shorts, no loud offensive T-shirts and the proper safety gear is worn as the job dictates.

While this list is by no means exhaustive I would strongly recommend that you adopt your own 'code of practice' for your business, particularly if you have others working for you.

Small talk can damage your business

Be aware of how idle chat and throwaway remarks can affect your client's decision as to whether they employ your services or use the competition. Maintaining and creating a professional image means you don't bring your personal opinions or prejudices to your client's doorsteps.

A few months ago I decided we could no longer put off having a section of our roof retiled. So I began to look for any recently re-tiled roofs in our area, find one that looked professionally done and get whoever did it to come and give me a quote. It wasn't long before I found a house with a well-finished roof. Outside was a board advertising the services of the roofer who carried out the job. I phoned him up and this is what happened:

The first time I phoned there was no answer. Neither was there on the following four occasions. Thinking I'd written the number down incorrectly, I revisited the house. The number I'd been dialling was correct. I tried again. The phone was answered, but by a child. I love children but there's nothing worse than having to do business with them. Eventually, I managed to convince the child to put her parent on.

"Allo?'

'Is this so and so roofing?'

'Eh, whose calling?' The nicotine stained voice sounded as if she was about to rip my head off.

'Em, well I was wondering whether or not you could come around and have a look...' I was cut dead.

'Hang on. I'll get him for you.'

I knew I should have hung up but I didn't. While I waited for 'him' to come to the phone I was entertained by the sounds of the television, dog and child. Finally, he came to the phone and after a few minutes of him sounding me out, I think making sure I wasn't an undercover tax man he agreed to come and look at my roof. He failed to keep the first appointment but he did phone two hours after it to tell me he'd got caught up with something. We made another appointment and this time he turned up on time. He began by telling me that the reason he didn't turn up the last time was because he'd been doing a bit of business. His friend's boat was for sale for £2,000 and when one of my roofer's clients told him they were looking for a boat, he mentioned he had one for sale. Not his friend, but him. He took his client to see the boat and told him it was £2,500, but he could do them a special price of £2,300. His client agreed. He then offered his friend, who he knew was short of cash, £1,500 for the boat. His friend agreed. My future roofer bought and sold the boat making a cool £800 while never actually owning it. Prior to this I was having great doubts about using him, and having heard how he'd ripped his friend and client off, I had now decided.

He then spent no more than a couple of minutes looking at my roof from ground height before exclaiming: 'For cash, £400.'

Needless to say, I didn't use him.

Businesses run in this fashion, with clients treated with contempt, are not uncommon. Rather than become frustrated and angry that Mr Roofer expects us to pay our taxes, and all the rest, while he'll happily take all that's going and pay as little as possible to the state, we should see him as a positive sign that there were always be room in the market for a professional well-run business.

Standing out from the crowd

Imagine that you are the one looking for a gardener to do some work in your garden. You don't know of anyone personally, so you have to set about finding a suitable gardener.

Opening the *Yellow Pages*, *Thompson Directories* and the classified section of your local paper, you're faced with a bewildering choice of companies. So where do you start? Probably you'll do what the majority of people do, and scan the advertisements for someone who appears to be professional and lists in their ad whatever you need to have done.

In my opinion most people will avoid the 'Beat any price – guaranteed' merchants. Neither will they rush off to phone anyone with 'We're the best, stuff the rest', type of message, especially when no evidence is offered to support their assertion. Of course were the advertisement to read:

BJ Landscaping Company
Gold Medal Winner Chelsea Flower Show 2002
RHS Diploma, Dip Hort
Tel – 000 000000

this would certainly indicate that the company not only had horticultural qualifications but had also achieved an enviable award. But don't be surprised if when you phone up such a business they tell you they're booked out for the rest of the season.

Selecting a suitable business from pages of advertisements is a difficult task which most people will go to great lengths to avoid.

Now imagine you're driving home from work one evening and you see a clean, tidy vehicle, tastefully sign-written with the name of a gardening company. You stop and take a further look and you see gardener at work trimming a hedge. You note that at each end of where they are working they have placed warning signs: **Caution – Hedge Trimming in Progress**. You're even more impressed when you notice that the gardener is suitably attired and not dressed like a football hooligan. It's likely that this is the company you would ask to quote for your gardening requirements. Nothing beats a real, live demonstration.

> **You, and you alone, are your business's greatest advertisement. Whether you're cutting a hedge, laying turf, weeding or pruning roses, potential clients will be watching you. If you present yourself and your business in an impressive manner, this will generate far more business than you could ever expect from any expensive advertisement.**

Creating the right image means that you devote sufficient time and energy to appearances. This means:

♦ Dressing appropriately.

♦ Having your business name tastefully sign-written on your vehicle or, if this is not possible, having an advertisement board that you can place where you're working.

◆ Making sure that your tools are always clean and in good working order.

◆ Paying sufficient attention to the safety of everyone who may be at risk because of the work you are doing. These can include yourself, your client, passers-by, neighbours etc.

◆ Parking your vehicle where it doesn't cause unnecessary obstruction.

◆ Making sure you leave everywhere, especially any public footpath or road clean and tidy when you finish.

Generating sales enquiries

Don't rely solely on advertising to generate your sales enquiries.

The vast majority of my business comes from the following sources:

◆ existing clients
◆ client referrals
◆ being approached by a neighbour or passer-by while working at someone's garden.

I consciously avoid expensive advertising to make things happen in my business.

I believe the money spent on large adverts in expensive publications could be far better used in your business, for example having your van sign-written or investing in some time-saving tools. *By getting your outward appearance right, you will invite people to approach you when you're working and ask for your help.* Nothing beats having a complete stranger walks up to you when you're working one day and say: 'Excuse me, I've been really impressed with your gardening skills, I wonder are you available to do some gardening for me?'

This will happen time and time again provided you project the right image.

Business stationery

Is business stationery important and do you need it?

Business cards and letterhead

Whether or not you invest in a complete stationery suite will depend on:

- the type of business you're planning to run
- the size of your proposed business
- the services you offer
- whether or not you can initially afford to.

If you're planning a small local gardening round, one where you will quickly achieve a full diary, then I'd suggest you don't need a set of stationery. But for any other business I believe that a smart, crisp business card together with matching letterhead, is a necessity as opposed to a luxury.

Beware of doing it yourself

I believe there is nothing worse than a homemade business card. With the arrival of personal computer software it seems that everyone is now a graphic designer. Unfortunately, if what you see about is anything to go by, gardeners should stick to gardening and leave it to the professionals.

Even if what you manage to produce at home looks appealing, it won't stay that way for long. For as soon as you hand your card to your prospective client it will start its rapid descent towards dog-eared, ink splurged deterioration. *Professionally produced business cards don't just look better; they are made from quality materials including the ink.* The ink that we use in our PCs is certainly not designed to be used in documents that will spend some time outdoors in all weather, which is where you will be meeting most of your clients.

Printing booths

The alternative to having business cards printed by a high street printer is to use one of those instant printing booths. I think they're on a par with the machines that print your passport photo in terms of presentation and quality. They're fine for passports but that's it. Likewise instant business cards are great for notifying everyone of your change of address, summer barbeque, party or whatever. But they're pretty uninspiring if you're trying to convince potential clients that you're the person who is going to make or keep their garden beautiful.

Start-up packages

Most high street printers offer start-up stationery kits for small new businesses. While charges may vary, you should find that you can obtain a set of business cards, letterhead and compliment slips for under £100. Or if you opt for business cards alone, the damage should be no greater than £50. Considering the price you pay for DIY business card paper and the cost of your ink cartridge, I really do believe that it's cheaper to use a professional printer.

Before rushing off to the printers work out a number of different drafts of how your business card will look. Whatever you come up with, leave them alone for a few days before deciding which one you're going to have printed. If you are thinking of having a dedicated business line in your home but haven't yet arranged it, then obviously you need to wait until you get your number before having 200 cards printed.

Business cards are important. When you're working on someone's garden you'll be surprised how often neighbours will ask you for your card. Nothing is worse than handing your telephone number over written on the back of an envelope.

> But never simply hand your card over. You must always book an appointment there and then, whether to come and see what needs to be done, or better still a time to do the work.

When I first started I handed my cards out to everyone who asked me for one. Now I don't. Instead I offer them an appointment. People seldom refuse. After all it is they who have approached you. This is a great, cost-effective way of getting new clients. When I gave my cards out to all who asked for them I found the results disappointing.

There are a number of reasons why these initially very interested people don't call you. Often it's because they are not the decision-maker in their homes and when they tell their partner that they're thinking of hiring a gardener, you can imagine the response. Others simply lose your card, change their minds, didn't really need one, are working undercover for the Benefits Agency, Inland Revenue, local council and so on. *So if approached by anyone looking to hire you – book an appointment.*

Make your business cards earn their keep in your enterprise by putting them wherever people have to sit and wait, for example:

♦ hairdressing salons
♦ barber's shops

- supermarket noticeboards
- garden centres
- DIY stores
- dentists' and doctors' waiting rooms
- give some to your friends and ask them to put one up in their work canteen.

Your letterhead

Treat your letterhead as you would were you having a brochure. Have it done by a high street printer on a quality, bonded notepaper. I prefer to buy white A5 envelopes with windows in them. This way you don't have to waste time addressing envelopes. It also looks more professional. If you have an email address think carefully before having it printed on your letterhead. Only have it included if you're going to keep this email address in the long term, and if you're going to check your email box daily. I prefer not to include my email address on my business letterhead, but it's up to you.

Whatever you decide to use in the way of stationery, go for quality. You don't have to invest fortunes, but don't end up with something the texture and longevity of newspaper.

Bank accounts

Should you open a business bank account prior to starting?

There is **no legal requirement** for you to have a separate bank account from your ordinary bank account. Indeed, there is no requirement for you to have any bank account. If you decide to keep your money in a tin under the bed, recording the ins and outs of your account on a roll of toilet paper, in pencil, then you're not breaking any law.

Clearly, it would be in your best interests if you didn't keep your money in a tin and you maintained correct records. *My own opinion is that you do need a separate bank or building society account for your business.* Many of your clients will want to pay you by cheque and to tell them you only accept cash is not only unprofessional but might also invite an investigation from the Inland Revenue.

Could you use your personal account for your business?

Banks and building societies have certain restrictions on how you manage your personal accounts. Generally, you are not allowed to use your personal account for business use.

Instead you will be invited to apply for a separate business account. If you're trading as a sole trader, which will be the most common form of trading entity for the majority of gardening businesses then your business account will be in your name followed by your trading name, for example *Paul Power trading as Paul Power Landscape Gardening*.

> Most banks will offer you a period of free banking. This can be anything from six to 18 months, depending on which bank you choose and whether or not you need an overdraft or financing for your business.

Building societies have now entered the business market and appear keen to encourage new business accounts. Certainly many are now offering a far more imaginative account package than the high street banks, with accounts that pay a far more generous rate of interest on your money and if you need to borrow their charges on the whole appear lower.

Be sure to shop around

Treat your banking as you would any purchase. *Shop around and get the best possible deal.* Ask lots of questions and read all the bumf they give you carefully. Go straight for the kill and start with the small print. How much is banking with so and so going to cost you after the initial period of free grace? Compare charges, overdraft fees and everything else, before opening your account.

Despite the relatively high costs, I believe having a separate business account is necessary because:

♦ You know where you are on a day-to-day basis without having to wade through your personal statements.

♦ Bookkeeping and record-keeping are certainly made easier and, if you employ a bookkeeper, their fees may be reduced.

Here is a list of some of the things you should look for in your business bank package.

Bank checklist

- Initial free banking period, minimum 18 months.
- Or life-time free banking, provided you manage your account within certain pre-arranged limits.
- Debit card.
- Cheque book.
- Paying in book.
- Monthly statements.
- Twenty-four hour access to your account via the internet.
- Seven-day-a-week telephone banking service.
- Interest on your current account balance.
- Clearly defined cheque clearance cycle – how long will it take for what you lodge to arrive in your account?
- A genuine interest in small businesses – don't always go for what they say in their brochure.

Most business bank accounts will include the services of a relationship manager. Their sales literature will detail what this person can do for you, that he or she will take a special interest in both you and your business, and that they are as determined as you to see you succeed.

My experience has been something different. While my relationship manager was friendly, approachable and an all-round good egg, it was very clear to me after our first meeting that he was working for the bank and not for me. His interests in my business were limited to his bank's interests. The discussion we had concerning my banking needs largely centred around whether or not I had sufficient insurance and the like. I was left with the impression that his interest didn't go beyond that of selling me the bank's products.

When I actually needed the bank's help in the way of having a short-term overdraft to see me through what I had imagined was going to be a lean few months, my application was turned down. Every time I went into my branch to make a lodgement I was scarcely acknowledged by the morose staff.

The final straw came when I received a nice letter from the bank wondering whether I'd ever considered starting a business and that if I wanted an information pack on what they could for me, all I had to do was ask. Nothing was too much trouble for them. Having banked with this bank for over 11 years, I was appalled that they didn't even recognise I was one of their customers. To think of all the interest that I've paid in these years, not to mention the charges I pay for having my personal account with them. Enough was enough. It was time to change. I looked around at all the various packages available, and the organisation that satisfied the above criteria was the one that got my business. Relationship managers are a very nice idea, but don't you think if they knew half as much as they say they do about running a small business, they'd be doing it themselves?

I have now switched my business banking to a building society, where I not only enjoy a high rate of interest on any funds in my current account, but also free banking for life provided I maintain my account within certain pre-agreed guidelines.

> **Make sure you get the best deal possible when opening your bank account. Look beyond the introductory free banking offers and work out which bank or building society is giving you the best deal. Don't be afraid to shop around and ask lots of questions.**

Getting your first customers – the gardening round

Prepare an initial sales strategy

Whatever business you're planning to start – gardening round, lawn cutting round, general gardening company or any one of the many other businesses we've looked at, you'll need to have a clear sales strategy worked out prior to starting.

A gardening round is a unique business where a different approach is needed. This business is unique in that once your initial objective of finding enough clients to fill whatever diary space you have available is achieved, you will probably no longer need the same continued concentrated sales effort that the other businesses will require.

This is not to say that you should not be continually looking at ways of improving your sales figures and introducing new services and products to your market place. Barring unforeseen circumstances, provided you manage your round in a professional way, making every one of your clients feel as if they are your only one, then you should enjoy their custom for many years to come. You will only have to 'replace' your clients when they move on, by which time your reputation will hopefully be such that you have a good-sized waiting list of clients eager for you to come and work in their gardens.

However, you will still need an initial sales strategy. Here are some of the things that you will need to consider:

- geographical location of your round
- competition
- timing – when in the main season you start your round
- advertising – getting your clients.

Geographical location

It's essential you choose an area as close to where you live as possible. Once you have chosen this area it's then equally important that you try and keep your round as close as possible. This means making sure that the majority of your time is spent gardening as opposed to travelling. Easier said than done!

Existing competition – who is there already?

Unless you're very lucky, the area that you choose to work in will most probably have a number of gardeners with established rounds. This should not deter you. There will always be room for another professional.

- At the end of every season a number of gardeners hang their tools up for the last time and retire.

- Others finish for a variety of reasons including ill health, moving away from the area, change of personal circumstances.

- There will also be homeowners who didn't need the services of a regular gardener last year but now do.

So if you discuss your plans with anyone already living in your chosen area (something I strongly recommend you don't do), and they tell that you that there's no point in you trying to start there because so and so has already got the area sewn up, don't listen to them.

Timing – when to start

Ideally you should aim to launch this business in the spring. If this is not possible, and you find yourself having to start mid way though the summer don't despair. You will still find a market for your services.

> **At any one given time there will always be homeowners needing you.**

Some of the problems you may encounter if you start mid-way through the main season are:

◆ Difficulty finding sufficient clients in one particular area, which means increased, ie wasted travelling time spent between appointments.

◆ Generally the work you might be asked to do is that which the others have turned down, for example weeding. Many clients will already have someone to cut their lawn and trim their hedges, but can they find someone to weed? While certainly this is a sales opportunity in itself, weeding every day, all day is not something that is either enjoyable or good for you. Chances are if you end up with weed-only jobs you won't be in this business for very long.

◆ If you're planning to work at this business full-time, the sooner you fill your diary with work the better. A slow start will have a negative impact on your cash flow and depending on how late in the season you start, it might be the following year before you've enough clients to make it profitable.

Getting your round up and running

There are many different ways of advertising your services, but in my experience nothing will make this happen faster than if you place a number of well presented advertisement cards in a whole range of local outlets, especially newsagents.

If you think advertising your business in a newsagent's window is amateurish and unprofessional you can be forgiven.

When I first considered using this medium I dismissed it as completely inappropriate. Who in their right mind would employ anyone who advertises their business like this? I couldn't have been more wrong. Despite my enormous concerns, I decided to place a number of cards in a few local newsagents. A fortnight later, when I hadn't received any calls, I decided to do things properly and placed a large, expensive advertisement in my local paper. The day after the advertisement was published my phone started ringing. Naturally I was delighted with the response, and my only regret was that I'd bothered to waste my time with the newsagents. I couldn't have been more wrong, for it was only when I met my first callers that they mentioned they'd seen my ads in their newsagents. Ironically, none of them had come via my expensive newspaper ad. In fact, in the six weeks the newspaper ad was running I only received one call, and even this enquiry failed to generate an order.

While it might appear that there is something almost unprofessional doing it this way, the facts are that:

- In many neighbourhoods the newsagent is still a respected, trusted local business. While generally newsagents don't vet their advertisers, there is nevertheless a belief that if the newsagent has accepted your card then you must be okay. To an extent this is true. I have known cases where the newsagent has withdrawn his advertiser's card because of complaints he's received from his customers. How many magazine publishers would do this?

- Gardeners have a long tradition of advertising their services in shop windows and for those looking for one this is the most obvious first port of call.

- Newsagents' windows enjoy wide exposure. It's difficult not to browse through the classifieds even if you're not looking for anything.

But the greatest benefits to your business of using this system is that:

- It is cheap and effective – a rare combination.

- It's instant. You don't have to wait until the publication you are advertising in reaches the shops. Hand your card over, pay your money and your ad is in the window for everyone to see 24 hours a day, seven days a week. You can target your advertising to particular areas and neighbourhoods.

- You can either increase or reduce your advertisements instantaneously, seven days a week.

> If you have any reservations about how successful this method of advertising is, then I would ask you to put them aside until you have given it a try. Believe me, it works. It's a terrific way of kick-starting your round in the area that you wish to operate in. And it's hugely cost-effective.

You will still need to be careful how you approach this.
Just because you're advertising in a shop window doesn't mean that your advertisement should be any less eye-catching, or less informative, than if you were advertising in a glossy magazine. Nothing looks worse than a hastily scribbled ad on a piece of card supplied by the shop. You'll need to do much more than that. Give some thought to the layout of your cards. Make sure that:

◆ Cards are not handwritten. Nothing looks worse than a hastily written note. You can either print them at home on your computer, or if you haven't got a PC have someone do them for you.

◆ Whatever is printed is clear and easily read from a distance. Use too small a font size and no one will be able to make out what it is you're offering.

◆ Your name and telephone number are printed at the bottom of your ad, and are larger than the rest of the information. It's crucial that anyone interested in employing you can interpret your telephone number correctly.

◆ Do not use a mobile telephone number. Many of the people for whom I have worked have told me that under no circumstances would they consider employing someone who does not have a land based telephone number. If you're worried that you might lose calls when you're not at home, then either re-direct your home telephone number to your mobile, or alternatively have two numbers printed on your card.

◆ Don't cram your card with too much text. Keep it to a minimum but make sure you include the important words: 'Fully insured', and that if you already have gardened for someone be it a friend, colleague or whoever, and they were pleased with what you did, you include: 'References available'.

◆ Stick your card to some cardboard before asking the shopkeeper to put it up for you.

◆ Don't put your prices on your card or any other sales literature that you may print.

Here's what my first card looked like:

PROFESSIONAL GARDENER AVAILABLE
Regular Gardening Work Undertaken
Hedge Trimming
Weeding
Lawn Cutting
Seasonal Pruning
Overgrown Gardens Cleared
Telephone Paul on
12121212
Fully Insured, References Available

When putting your cards up make sure that you:

◆ Place your cards in all of the newsagents in the area you wish to work.

◆ Keep a diary record of the date your card goes in the window. Make a further diary entry no later than two days before the ad is due to be removed to give you sufficient time to renew it if necessary.

◆ Initially, at least, pay to have your cards up for a full calendar month.

◆ Keep a regular eye on the newsagents to make sure that they are still displaying your card. My experience was that occasionally my cards would either fall down, or be taken down in error prior to their expiry date.

Don't just limit your advertisement cards to newsagents.

Put them up anywhere people will see them, provided of course you're not breaking any law.

Alternatives to using cards to launch your business.

If under no circumstances will you consider putting up advertising cards, or you live in area where there are no newsagents who you will allow you to, then you will have to use some of the strategies that follow for launching your business.

Remember though that the gardening round is a unique business in itself. It's one of those enterprises where you will visit your clients on either a weekly, fortnightly or once monthly cycle. *Your first business objective must be to fill your diary quickly without incurring a large advertising bill in the process.* Provided you give a professional service you will have no difficulty achieving this. Future expansion will be based on personal recommendations.

> The most important thing for you to do is to find your first client without having to invest fortunes in time and money.

Launch strategy for other businesses

Sales forecasting

One of the most difficult things for any businessperson contemplating launching a business is predicting how quickly initial sales targets can be achieved. While it may be difficult, it is not impossible. Don't be tempted to shy away from producing a sales forecast that not only includes your first three months of trading, but first complete year.

In Chapter 2 we looked at preparing a sales forecast as part of your business plan. If you haven't already done so, I strongly recommend that you take the time needed to prepare one for your proposed venture.

My favoured way of forecasting is to prepare three:

1. Sales forecast predicting a worst case scenario.
2. Sales forecast predicting a best case scenario.
3. Sales forecast predicting the most likely scenario.

Normally, you would hope to accomplish sales forecast number 2, but would be prepared for and satisfied with forecast number 3. Of course the worst-case scenario should be avoided at all costs. However, I believe it a very useful, if not vital exercise that you prepare a worst-case forecast, because by doing so you are made to focus on what you will need to do to avoid it. This makes your initial sales strategy far more effective and concentrated.

A word on positive thinking

While I'm all for having a positive outlook and believing that if you believe in yourself you can achieve anything you want, I also think it of the utmost importance that you do not adopt an 'it'll be alright on the night' philosophy when it comes to planning your new venture. There's too much to risk. *Don't rely on faith and circumstances being kind to you. Work out how you are going to achieve your sales.* Produce as many sales forecasts as you need to before deciding on which one is the right one for your business. Remember you must plan to succeed. Accept nothing less from yourself and don't leave things to chance.

Guidelines for preparing your sales forecast

♦ Be optimistic, but realistic. Success will only be possible if what you're planning is achievable.

♦ Give yourself an initial **period of grace**. Ideally, you should allow yourself your first month of trading as a zero sales month. This will take some of the pressure off and allow you to concentrate on generating business for the following month. Remember that starting and running your own business will include working on sales as well as trimming hedges and cutting lawns!

♦ **Timing** – if you're going to start your business in time for spring or autumn (times when your services will be most in demand), you should launch your business at least one month in advance of this period.

♦ **Survival income** – initially, it may be that you will not earn enough to cover your survival income. Provided you anticipate this in your forecasting and make adequate provision for having enough capital to see you through this period then you should have no problem. Your forecast must include the month when you plan to earn enough to cover your survival income and once achieved your sales should not fall below this figure.

♦ **Profit**. Don't forget it. It's an important part of why you're in business. There is little point being in business if your sole objective is to simply pay yourself a wage. If this is the case then you may as well work for someone else. To succeed, your business must earn a profit. The month you anticipate your business will reach the point of being profitable must be included in your forecast.

Getting the phone to ring

This is what it's all about – getting your phone to ring with a regular flow of callers, eager for you to come and work for them. Achieve this, and you're in business, literally!

In my experience, sitting around waiting for the phone to ring is the most soul-destroying experience of all. It's a bit like filling a kettle and waiting for it to boil, it seems to take forever. By far the most rewarding thing you can do is be proactive.

> **Don't wait for things to happen – make them happen.**

Some of the ways you can kick-start sales without relying on advertising are to:

- offer your services free of charge to a favourite local charity
- canvass for business
- attend exhibitions or craft fairs
- offer sponsorship
- attract press interest.

Services free of charge

There are lots of well-deserving causes that would greatly appreciate your offer of help to either prepare or make over an overgrown area of their garden for free. You could donate anything from a day of your time to a week. Believe me the amount of referral business you can get from doing something like this is enormous. And you're helping a worthwhile cause in the process.

> I like to do this as a matter of course, not just as a way of drumming up new business, but also as a way of giving something back.

Canvass for business

This is where you directly sell your business in your chosen area. Dress appropriately, arm yourself with enough leaflets and get out there knocking on doors asking for gardening work. Make sure you bring your diary with you to book the appointment to have the work done when the householder is an agreeable mood.

If no one's in, then post a leaflet through their door. If and when you come across the properties that are adorned with an arrangement of warning signs, then my advice is to walk past them. Even if whoever lived there did actually open the door, your welcome could be such that you'd be put off calling on anyone else's door.

Direct selling is a positive way of promoting your business. If you get out there and do it, you'll be surprised at how quickly you can fill your diary. Remember all you need to do is to establish yourself with one client in any given area to start getting valuable reference work. Again, you are your business' best advertisement.

Exhibitions or craft fairs

Rent a stall at a local craft fair or exhibition. If you really want to kick-start your new venture and you're not afraid of jumping in at the deep end, this is a great way of filling your diary with appointments. Make sure that you have sufficient leaflets printed and give one to everyone who visits your stall.

Your stand will need to have some sort of inviting, interesting display to attract people to it to begin with. If your own garden is up to it, you could photograph it and exhibit the pictures. My favourite way of attracting attention is to create a miniature garden complete with real turf and water feature. With a little imagination this can be achieved relatively easily. *It will provide a wonderful talking point and will certainly give you an opportunity to sell your business.*

Sponsorship

If you're unable to offer your services free of charge to a local charity, you could consider sponsoring a flowerbed, window box or similar. Have a little plaque made up with your business name and telephone number on it and fix it to the bed or box.

You could also sponsor individuals who are doing something on behalf of a local or national charity.

Attracting press interest

In my experience local papers are generally very approachable when it comes to finding some free publicity for your business, provided your offering has an interesting twist, or your business is unique in some way. There's little point in phoning up the editor of your local paper and telling him you're about to launch your own gardening business. His only action will be to pass you on to the classified sales section to sell you some advertising space. But were you the local council's head gardener either leaving or retiring from your post to start up your business then in all probability the editor would be interested in your story. *If you're stuck for ideas on what would make your business newsworthy, then think about the reasons why you're starting it. There's a news story lurking there somewhere.* All you have to do is dig it out!

Advertising

I believe that traditional advertising can have a place in your business, provided that you do not expect your ad to do all the work for you. If you find that during a certain period your phone is not ringing, then don't be tempted to place as many advertisements in as many publications as you can afford. This doesn't work. You need to understand why your phone is not ringing. Here are some of the most common reasons:

♦ Half-term and school holidays. Many of your clients will either go away during these times, or if they stay at home will not want to have their holiday disrupted.

♦ Public holidays such as Easter and Christmas. Again many people go away.

♦ August – generally the quietest month of the year for new enquiries. Again it is a popular holidaying month, but it's also a quiet time in the garden compared with the rest of the year. Obviously those with gardening rounds or lawn-cutting rounds will still have ample to do, but don't be surprised if your telephone isn't as busy during this month.

Where to place regular advertisements

There are literally hundreds of publications where you can advertise your business including:

♦ directories – *Yellow Pages, Thompsons Directory*
♦ local newspapers
♦ magazines
♦ local specialist publications
♦ web sites
♦ radio stations.

Directories

Running an ad in a directory is not a cheap option. It has certain advantages in that:

◆ Your ad is available to a wide audience.

◆ Most households have these directories somewhere even if they're only being used as door stoppers.

However, there are a number of disadvantages with this type of advertising:

◆ Relatively expensive.

◆ You can't start advertising mid-way through the year. Start your business in the spring and it won't be until the following year that your entry is published.

◆ If you're going to use this medium your advertisement would have to be sufficiently large enough not to be dwarfed by the other ads.

◆ The area the directory covers is generally larger than the area the average one-person gardening business will cover. You could find yourself with a steady stream of callers from outside your local area who you are unable to help.

◆ If you're planning to work part-time or have a seasonal business you will want to have more control over your advertising, ie, stopping your ad when you down tools for the winter.

I wouldn't recommend directories as a suitable medium for newcomers. My advice would be to run your business for at least a year before you consider placing an advertisement, by which time you will have a clear idea on the direction you would like your business to take and will be in a better position to formulate an effective, targeted advertising campaign.

Local newspapers

These fall into two categories:

◆ free papers
◆ those you buy weekly from your newsagents.

I can't say that I am particularly keen on using either to advertise my business. The main reasons are:

◆ Relatively expensive.

◆ Generally there are a lot of gardeners advertising their services here. Why should anyone choose you as opposed to the advertisement above you?

◆ Because this is a weekly paper your advertisement may well end up wrapping fish and chips by lunchtime the day following its publication.

If you are keen to advertise in your local paper then I would recommend you:

◆ Have your advertisement inserted somewhere other than in the gardening classified section. If the paper runs a weekly gardening column (many now do), try to have your ad placed on the same page.

◆ Property pages are one of the better places to advertise. Word your advertisement to target those selling their houses who could benefit by employing your skills to give it a good tidy up to ensure a better price, or those who've just acquired a property who could use your services.

◆ You must advertise for a minimum period of three months. Anything less and those who have seen your ad will imagine you've gone out of business if your details no longer appear.

Give this option some serious thought before you place your advertisement. It can be a very expensive mistake if you get it wrong. Beware also of advertising in freebie newspapers that are hand-delivered, as delivery isn't always reliable. The rates paid to delivery people are fairly miserable which encourages a fair amount of papers being mass delivered to a convenient bin or skip.

Magazines

I am a fan of magazine advertising, provided of course that the magazine enjoys a sufficient circulation to make it worthwhile. Where I live we have a number of quality magazines that are only available in our area. The fact that these magazines are targeted at local interest ensures that when you advertise your business in them you're reaching your targeted audience.

I maintain an ongoing monthly ad in one of these magazines and have been rewarded with a steady stream of quality business. I'm also fortunate that I am the only gardening company to advertise in my chosen publication.

If you are fortunate to live in an area where you have local, quality magazines then I would recommend you consider placing an ad. As in newspaper advertising, you will have to leave your advertisement in for a number of months before it starts paying dividends; certainly nothing less than three months to begin with, and if during this trial period you find it successful make sure that you negotiate a discount for placing a regular ad.

Local specialist publications

There are an untold number of specialist publications being published in communities all around the country, ranging from drama societies to floral arranging club newsletters. These represent an excellent opportunity for anyone launching a new gardening business or looking to expand an existing one.

Many of these publications are classified as newsletters as opposed to magazines. You may wonder why a gardener would wish to advertise his or her services in the local golf club's publication, but it is here that you will find a ready market for your services. Most golfers that I know would agree with me when I say that keen golfers will do anything to get out of spending their free time gardening when they could be golfing. Don't worry if the circulation appears low when compared to other mainstream publications. Advertising rates usually reflect this. The rewards can be enormous for advertising in these publications.

Good areas of publications to advertise in include:

- church newsletters
- chess society newsletters
- sailing club newsletters
- local companies' in-house magazines or newsletters
- any publication whose intended readership is amongst the retired or newly-weds
- local sports clubs' publications
- many private gyms now publish newsletters keeping their clients up-to-date with the latest in health and fitness.

Web sites

I'm not convinced that this is the best place for a new gardening company to advertise their services. While this medium is most suitable for a garden design company to showcase their work, it isn't necessarily going to give you wide exposure unless you follow up with a traditional print based advertisement, which gives details of your web site address. If your business is going to have to rely on potential clients using search engines to find you, then you stand little chance of getting the wide exposure needed to make it successful.

While gardening sites may be mushrooming all over the net, this isn't necessarily a good thing for your business. Try putting the word 'gardener' into your favourite search engine and you'll see what I mean.

The alternative is that you place an advertisement with an already established local directory or magazine web site. Some sites charge for the privilege, others are happy to give your business a free listing. I wouldn't recommend you pay to advertise your business on the web, but by all means take advantage of any free listing that's going.

> **Whether you decide to advertise your business in a newspaper, magazine, web site or whatever is a choice only you can make. Don't feel that you have to. Many successful businesses are started and established without ever having to pay for advertising. Nothing will fill your diary quicker than getting out in your locality and introducing your business yourself.**

Summary

♦ Make sure you do sufficient groundwork before starting your business. Presentation and planning are just as important to the success of your business as enthusiasm.

♦ Never undercut current market prices, or you will not be long in business.

♦ When selling remember the golden rule – *people buy benefits not features.*

♦ Wherever possible try to get to know your competitors. There is no reason why you should be enemies or fear them. You may even find them willing to help you out when you're stretched and vice versa.

◆ Creating a positive image is vital to your success. Often it's the small talk that kills future orders. Beware of volunteering opinions. Your job is to offer a quality gardening service, not commentate on current affairs. It's easy to insult people without knowing you're doing it. So be careful what you say and to whom.

◆ Always make your client feel as if they are your only one.

◆ When opening a bank of building society account, make sure you shop around and get the best deal.

CHAPTER SEVEN

Bookkeeping and Administration Systems

All about keeping track of your growing finances.

Tax for the self-employed

Keeping records

Surely nothing could be worse than arriving home after a hard day's work and then having to plough through lots of paperwork, especially work involving figures?

> I used to detest bookkeeping. It was one of those tasks that I kept putting off until eventually I had no choice but to either do the books or the books would do me. If you think otherwise, then think again. When you find yourself knee deep in receipts, but can't find the one you're looking for, it is then that you really start wishing you had spent some time getting organised.

It doesn't have to be a chore.

> Now I don't find bookkeeping the awful chore it used to be. By doing it on a regular basis, I've found that it takes little or no time. Since taking an interest in the financial wellbeing of my business, I've found that keeping costs down has become easier, as has pricing new work.

Keeping a close eye on expenditure is only possible if you maintain a regular record.

Accurate, up-to-the-minute books are invaluable when making business decisions. You must prioritise your bookkeeping. Doing it regularly will not only save you time but also make the whole exercise less of a chore and focus you on the two most important issues facing your business — earnings and expenditure.

If you're still not convinced here are some powerful reasons for making sure that you keep accurate records of your business income and expenditure:

♦ You are legally required to keep a record of all your business income and expenditure.

♦ You must be able to substantiate your accounts, or in your case, your annual tax return. This means not only must you record all your business income and expenditure, but also keep receipts. *Without accurate, up-to-date records you cannot really be sure how well your business is doing, or accurately determine what you need to do to improve your performance.*

Legal trading identity

In Chapter 2 we looked at the various legal entities that you could use for your business:

♦ sole trader
♦ partnership
♦ limited company.

Whatever trading entity you choose will be determined by a number of factors such as if you're planning to work alone or with another person.

Most businesses will be operated as either a sole trader or partnership. In my opinion there is no benefit in forming a limited company from which to operate, however this will depend on your own personal circumstances and aspirations.

If you are planning to form a limited company for your business you will no longer be operating as a self-employed person but as an employee of the company that you formed. Directors of limited companies are still PAYE workers. In addition your company will be liable to pay corporation tax and you will have to have a number of additional legal obligations in relation to the preparation and auditing of your year-end accounts.

If you are planning to form a limited company for your business you should take professional advice prior to starting.

Sole trader/partnerships

These are by far the most appropriate trading entities for this type of business. For the purpose of calculating tax, you are classified as self-employed.

Your legal responsibilities as a self-employed person:

- You must register as self-employed within three months of starting your business.

- You must pay Class 2 National Insurance contributions. These are normally paid monthly by direct debit. These contributions count towards incapacity benefit, state retirement pension and bereavement benefit.

- By registering as a self-employed person you are responsible for paying your own tax. Every April your tax office will send you a self-assessment tax return, which you must complete and return. You have the option of either calculating your own tax, or if you wish filling out the form and requesting your tax office to calculate your tax for you. If you wish to do the latter, you must have your return to your tax office no later than 30 September.

- You must keep a record of all your business expenditure and business income, and keep these records for at least five years from the latest date for sending back your tax return.

If you're preparing to run a part-time business alongside either a current full or part-time job, where you are classified as an employee, ie, you are a PAYE worker, then effectively you will be an employee and self-employed at the same time. Thus you have the same responsibilities of any self-employed person.

When registering as a self-employed person you will need to:

1. Register with the Inland Revenue for National Insurance purposes. You are liable for Class 2 contributions from the moment you begin self-employment. The number to call is 08459 154515.

2. Contact your local Tax Office and inform them that you are now self-employed. They will then send you your self-assessment tax form every April.

    When I started I made the mistake of registering only with the Contributions Office. It was only the following April, when I phoned to query why my self-assessment form had failed to arrive that I was told that you need to inform both.

Value Added Tax

What is VAT?

VAT is a tax levied on most goods and services that you buy. Certain goods are VAT exempt, for example education and training. There are three rates of VAT:

◆ 17.5%, which is the **standard rate**. As the name implies this is the most common rate

◆ 5% – **reduced rate**

◆ 0% – **zero rate**.

How does VAT affect your business?

When you purchase goods and services for your business, the price you pay will normally include an element of VAT, usually 17.5%.

Example
John Kavanagh buys a new lawnmower for his business — Kavanagh Garden Co. He pays £293.75 and is given a receipt. The receipt details the transaction and records the price of the machine, the amount of VAT that has to be paid and finally the total figure.

J French Garden Machinery Company

Receipt

Kavanagh Garden Co

Finches Lodge

Anytown

UK SM1

1 Quick Cut 17″ Lawnmower	£250
VAT @17.5%	£ 43.75
Total	£293.75

Paid In full. With thanks

John's purchase includes £43.75 of VAT. If John is *VAT registered* he can claim this money back from the government.

But, and there is a but:

If you are VAT registered you can normally reclaim the VAT on business purchases that you have made. These can include goods and services. However, you must also charge VAT on your goods and services.

This means that you will have to charge VAT on your services. This is called **output tax.** The VAT that you pay on goods and services that you pay is known as **input tax.**

Initially it may appear to be an attractive prospect to be able to claim back the VAT on all you buy. However, every sale that you make in your business is now subject to VAT, which may mean that you lose your competitive advantage.

Should your business be VAT registered?

Initially it may seem attractive. My own opinion is that there is no great advantage to being VAT registered. Before deciding here are some issues to consider:

◆ If you are VAT registered you will have to charge VAT on all your labour costs. This means adding 17.5% onto your bills.

◆ You will also incur additional bookkeeping as you will need to calculate your monthly or quarterly input and output taxes and either pay any tax due or collect your rebates.

◆ If your business is solely concerned with working for the domestic market, then by
   adding VAT you are in effect increasing your prices by 17.5%, which is a significant
   amount. Doing so could make your rates uncompetitive.

◆ If you are planning to work in the commercial market, ie business to business, you
   will find that a number of your clients' businesses will be VAT registered, which
   means that they can reclaim the VAT element of your invoice, thus reducing their
   bill.

**Whether or not you register your business for VAT really depends on what market you are
planning to work in.** If you're going to work primarily in the domestic market, being VAT
registered can make your prices uncompetitive. On the other hand, if you're planning to
work in the commercial market many of your clients may be able to claim back the VAT
element of your invoice.

Deciding whether or not to register for VAT (known as voluntary registration) is
something that you will need to decide. However, the vast majority of gardening
businesses, which supply labour as their primary service, will not be VAT registered, as
there are no clear advantages for them doing so. But if at any time your annual turnover
exceeds a certain limit, known as a VAT threshold, then your business must be VAT
registered.

> Each year in the budget the government sets a VAT threshold for businesses. This means that
> when you reach or exceed this limit, you must register for VAT. Currently this threshold is
> £54,000. You only need to register when you reach this figure.

Bookkeeping – the options

There are a number of ways that you can tackle your bookkeeping:

◆ purchase a readymade manual bookkeeping system
◆ purchase a readymade computer software package
◆ create your own systems
◆ employ a professional bookkeeper to do it for you.

Readymade manual system

Of all the options this is my favourite in terms of both simplicity and cost effectiveness. You'll find a number of readymade manual bookkeeping systems on sale in your local high street stationers. The one that I use in my business is called *The Best Small Business Accounts Book, For a Non-VAT Registered Small Business*. The system contains:

♦ monthly sales record
♦ monthly expenditure record
♦ monthly bank record
♦ petty cash monitor.

This really is a simple but very effective way of keeping business records and providing you with all the information you need to complete your annual tax return.

The advantages to using this system are:

♦ Easy to use and comes complete with step-by-step instructions together with all the information you need to do your own bookkeeping.

♦ Relatively cheap.

♦ Your accounts are contained in one book as opposed to a number of different ones.

♦ Everything is provided to enable you to complete your annual tax return.

♦ If your business is VAT registered there is a specific account book for your business – *For a VAT Registered Small Business*.

You don't have to use this particular publication. I like it because it is so easy to use and relatively inexpensive. Most quality high street stationers will have a number of readymade manual bookkeeping systems on display. Choose the one you feel most suited to your needs.

Readymade computer software program

The advantages to using a computer software program is that again everything is done for you. Most programs now include profit and loss forecasting based on your performance, which is obviously helpful for your business planning. You can also print out invoices, receipts, month end reports etc.

I favour the manual system, as I believe it is more than adequate for my business and it costs substantially less.

Creating your own system

I cannot really see any advantage to you creating your own system. Even if you're only planning to work a half-day a week, I still believe it's more cost effective to purchase a readymade manual system. But if you really want to go it alone then here's what you're going to have to create – a system capable of recording:

♦ your income
♦ your expenditure
♦ the amount of money you pay into your bank account
♦ the amount of cash you keep in your office for small expenses (petty cash).

The easiest way to achieve this is to record both your income and expenditure in the same cash book. Divide the page up into two, devoting one side of the page to income and the other to expenditure.

Income
You will need to record:

♦ The date you received the money.
♦ The sales invoice number.
♦ Who the money was from.
♦ Whether payment was by cash or cheque.
♦ How much money you paid into the bank.

Expenditure
You will need to record:

♦ The date of the expenditure.
♦ Who you paid.
♦ How you paid. If by cheque the cheque number. If by credit card a note to this effect. If you paid by petty cash a note to this effect.
♦ The total amount you paid.

- The description of what you paid, for example petrol, insurance, telephone.

I would advise that if you are using your own system you complete monthly records. At the end of every month you will have the following information to hand:

- How much you earned from sales.

- How much you spent, including a breakdown or analysis of what you spent your money on. Thus in any given period you readily see how much you spent on petrol, postage, telephone etc. This information is essential if you are to use your accounts for anything other than helping you to complete your annual return.

Employing a professional

If you really don't want anything to do with books or bookkeeping then you could employ a bookkeeper. But if you wish to do this, don't forget that *you will still have to give your bookkeeper something that records both your income and expenditure for the given period.* You don't fully get away with the task of keeping records. If you intend to keep all your receipts in a plastic bag and hand them to your bookkeeper at the end of the year, then don't expect this service to come cheap. Neither will this be particularly effective as your bookkeeper, no matter how experienced, can only provide you with accounts based on what you provide them!

If you are a sole trader wishing to complete your annual tax return, you do not need to produce accounts to trial balance stage. You only need to provide an accurate, true reflection of the amount of money you earned and spent.

Whatever system or method you decide to use you will need to manage your accounts on a day-to-day basis.

Sales

You will need to:

- Provide your client with either an invoice or a receipt for each sale.
- Retain a copy of whichever document you use.

I prefer to raise an invoice for every sale I make and present this to my client when the work is completed. When the client settles the account, I mark their copy of the invoice as paid.

Invoices

You have two choices when it comes to invoices:

◆ Purchase a duplicate invoice book from an office supply company or high street stationer.

◆ Design your own and either print it using your PC or have a printer print a batch for you.

For both cost effectiveness and efficiency I use pre-printed duplicate invoice books, available in most stationers. These are inexpensive and there's no filing of invoices to do. After the sale, the copy remains in the original book.

Receipts

You do not have to issue a receipt for every payment you receive. However, it is important that you provide your customers with written confirmation that they have settled your account. My favoured way of doing this is to mark their copy of the invoice 'Paid with thanks' and date the entry. If you would prefer to issue a receipt then I recommend that purchase a duplicate receipt book from a high street stationers.

I always have available both my duplicate invoice book and duplicate receipt book. Although I rarely use the latter, there are circumstances which require both books.

Purchases

In addition to recording your purchases in your account book you will need a system for retaining all receipts. *Remember that if you wish to include any business expenditure in your accounts, you must have a receipt to substantiate the expenditure.*

There are various systems for doing this, ranging from stuffing every receipt you get into a drawer until the times comes when the drawer is overflowing, or your annual tax return is due, to using complex filing systems. The method I use, which is cheap and effective is to:

- Devote an A4 ring binder to each year's accounts.

- Insert 12 plastic A4 wallets into the binder. Stick a label on each wallet for each month.

- Whenever you make a business purchase, file the receipt in the corresponding month.

This really is a simple way of filing your receipts. At the end of the year you will have all of your expenditure neatly filed in month order. If you ever need to find a receipt quickly, then it's easy. Just go to the appropriate month.

Completing your annual tax return

Your annual tax return will arrive on your doorstep in April. Provided you have either maintained a ready-made record keeping system, or one you have created yourself, completing your return should be relatively straightforward. But if you find difficulties with any of the questions, the Inland Revenue provide a telephone helpline for advice.

> I have used this in the past and have found the staff to be extremely helpful and willing, no matter how many times I've called!

Getting paid everytime and on time

Payment terms

Generally, if you are working in the domestic market payment is requested when the job you've been asked to do is complete. You would not normally extend credit terms to your customers. I recommend that you include a small paragraph in your written quotations, estimations or confirmation letters covering the following payment terms:

- **Method of payment.** Are you going to accept cash only? Or cash and cheques? You don't have to accept cheques. My opinion is that you should accept cheques, but the choice is yours. If you are not going to accept cheques then you must inform your client of this prior to starting any work. Failure to do this will only lead to problems when you present your invoice.

◆ **Timing of payment.** Normally payment is due after the job is finished and your customer satisfied that everything he is being asked to pay for is completed.

Late payers

There can be a number of reasons why your customer will be unable to settle your account on the day you finish the job, the most common one being that they aren't physically present. In such circumstances I have simply put my invoice through their letterbox when I've finished and have received a cheque in the post a few days later. This system has worked very well. However, what do you do if your customer either fails to pay, or tells you they won't pay?

Your initial approach when dealing with late payment should be:

1. Make sure that your client has received your invoice. The best way to do this is by way of a polite telephone call. No need to be aggressive or threatening. In fact, there will never be a need for you to be either of these things.

2. As soon as you've established that your client is in receipt of your invoice then you should ask them for payment.

3. If your client tells you that they will not be paying your invoice then obviously you'll need to know why. Perhaps they feel that you have not completed the initial job they asked you to do. Or they are not satisfied with your work. Obviously if this is the case you should return to their property and put right what needs to be put right. You can't charge someone for unfinished or below standard work (although there are many who do). If your client still refuses to pay follow the steps outlined later in this chapter Dealing with a payment dispute.

4. Assuming there is no dispute and if after your telephone call you have still not received payment, you should write to your client requesting they settle your account immediately. Make sure your letter is polite and enclose a copy of your invoice.

5. If payment is still not forthcoming you should write your client a final reminder letter. In this letter you advise your client that payment is now overdue and that unless your account is settled in full you will have no alternative but to take legal action to recover your debt.

If after this your account remains unpaid you have a number of options available to you:

◆ Instruct a debt recovery firm to write to your client requesting payment.

◆ Take them to court yourself.

> Prior to embarking on either route, you should ask yourself whether or not the outstanding debt is worth both the time and money required to recover it.

Debt recovery firms

On payment of a small fee you can instruct a debt recovery firm to recover the debt on your behalf. Provided that your client is not disputing your invoice, then a letter from one of these companies should be all that is needed to have your client settle your account. This is by far the easiest and most straightforward method of recovering a debt. If your client is still refusing to pay, then the firm you have employed will inform you of this and offer to recover the debt for you via the County Court. You will have to pay additional fees for this. It's at this point that you will have to decide whether or not it is worth chasing the debt, in terms of both time and money.

Taking your own legal action

Suing your client by issuing a County Court Summons is not particularly difficult, however you should first consider carefully:

◆ Have you the time available to complete paperwork and attend court hearings?

◆ If the dispute has arisen as a result of an allegation of poor workmanship, or you failing to do what you said you would, then your client will be given an opportunity to tell the court why he is not willing to settle your account. If the court rules in their favour, not only will you lose your legal fees but you could well up end paying your client's legal bill as well not being paid for the original job. Make sure that you have a concrete case before taking anyone to court.

♦ Is your invoice large enough to warrant this action? You will have to pay the court an initial fee to begin your action. If after the court serves a summons on your behalf and your client still refuses to pay, then you will have to pay further costs to arrange a court hearing.

Going ahead with your action

If you believe that you have a solid case and that the amount owed merits this action then suing your client is relatively straightforward:

♦ Find out the name and address of the County Court closest to where you live. You'll find them listed in the phone book under courts.

♦ Either phone up, or visit them to pick up an information pack together with the forms you will need to complete in order to begin your action.

♦ Complete the forms as per the court's instructions and enclose your payment. The court will then serve a summons on your client by first class post.

♦ Your client then has 14 days to reply to this summons.

♦ If your client fails to do anything you then ask the court for a judgement to be made immediately.

♦ If your client pays you then you simply inform the court that your action has been settled and that is the end of the matter.

♦ If your client acknowledges receipt of the summons and lodges a defence, then the court will send a copy of the defence to you. Both you and your customer must now complete questionnaires supplied by the court and return them to the court.

♦ Your claim will then be given a hearing date and you will be provided with directions from the court on what you must to do to prepare your case. It is at this point that you may have to pay additional costs.

♦ Finally, you will have to attend a hearing or trial.

Dealing with a payment dispute

Hopefully such instances will never arise. Certainly you can do a number of things to avoid disputes happening in the first place.

◆ Prior to starting any work you should always *send a written quote, estimate or confirmation* detailing what work you are proposing to carry out and at what price.

◆ *Communicate with your client.* If there is a problem with the job then let them know as soon as you do. Don't put in extra hours overcoming some obstacle that has arisen and then present your client with an inflated bill. If you're going to have to veer off your initial price then let your client know before carrying out the work.

If your client disputes your final bill then try to discuss the matter with them before threatening any legal action or demanding payment. Remember, if you do take your client to court for non-payment of your invoice, the court has a duty to listen to both sides. Just because you have initiated the action does not mean the court will necessarily rule in your favour.

If you find yourself deadlocked in a dispute then ask your client to put their complaint in writing. If they won't, then you should write to them as soon as possible outlining in your letter the steps you have taken to resolve their complaints. In the event of a court action you will need written evidence. Recollections of telephone discussions and meetings will most certainly be disputed. *So make sure you confirm and clarify everything in writing.*

> **Only when it appears to you that the matter cannot be resolved should you instigate legal action to recover a debt, and only then if it seems worthwhile.**

Staffing issues

Hiring additional help

There will be times in your business that you will need to hire some additional help either to help you with a specific job or to work with your during the busiest seasons. There are two ways to do this:

◆ use associates
◆ hire staff.

Associates

By far the easiest way of coping with additional work is for you to use associates.

- These are people who will work with you on a self-employed basis and at the end of the job, day or hour will provide you with an invoice for their labour at agreed rates. You then pay them and record the expenditure in your account book.

- They are responsible for paying their own tax and National Insurance.

- Even though they are self-employed, you must still have adequate Employers' Liability Insurance to cover them as they will be working under your direction.

> I have a network of associates I use in my business. It's an ideal way of having staff whenever you need them, without having to employ anyone full-time. I strongly recommend you consider using associates, at least to begin with.

Hiring staff

The most important thing to consider when deciding on hiring staff is making sure that you have enough work for them. Even one part-time staff member is an extra mouth for your business to feed. You also bring additional, and some would say onerous, responsibilities to your business:

- You will have to pay them whether or not you have the money available. It may happen that your wage bill will fall due before your clients have paid you. This may mean taking on an unnecessarily costly short-term bank overdraft facility.

- You are responsible for their health and safety and this means making sure that your employees are adequately trained to work in your business, which might mean additional training costs.

> The decision to take on employees in your business is one of the most important business decisions you are likely to make. As soon as you employ someone, even part-time, you become an employer. This means that you have legal duties and responsibilities to your employee or employees.

Your duties and responsibilities

Employment legislation is a complex subject and I recommend that if you are proposing to take on staff, other than using associates or sub-contractors, you undertake further research before doing so.

Your responsibilities will include that you must:

◆ Not discriminate when employing anyone on the grounds of sex, marital status, disability or race.

◆ Give your employee a written contract of employment within two months of starting.

◆ Tell your local tax office that you have taken on an employee.

◆ Deduct income tax and National Insurance from your employee's wages and pay this to the government.

◆ Pay where and when due, statutory sick pay and maternity pay.

◆ Provide your employee with statutory holiday leave – four weeks a year and pro-rata for part-time employees.

◆ Still be responsible for paying for your employee if you cannot work owing to bad weather.

◆ Ensure the health and safety of your employee whilst in your employment.

◆ Have a duty of care to all your employees.

◆ Pay the minimum wage and provide a payslip detailing pay and deductions.

◆ Give minimum notice periods as required by law if making someone redundant and pay redundancy money.

◆ Pay statutory maternity pay.

Taking on employees is a big step and one that you should consider carefully.

Where to get help

The Inland Revenue publish an invaluable New Employer Starter Pack, which can be obtained free of charge by telephoning their helpline on 0845 60 70 143 or visiting their web site at *www.inlandrevenue.gov.uk* and click on Employers. You can also contact their helpline for advice on the same number.

Summary

◆ Bookkeeping is an important part of your work. Accurate, up-to-the-minute books are vital for future business planning and looking at ways of improving performance.

◆ You are legally required to keep a record of all your business expenditure and income.

◆ Make sure that you choose the correct trading identity to begin with.

◆ When submitting your quotes and estimates, make sure you include a paragraph covering your payment terms, for example: *Payment in full is due on completion of the work and can be made by either cash or cheque.*

◆ Deciding to employ staff is one of the biggest business decisions you're likely to make. Be careful in the early days that you don't expand too quickly. Far better for you to be so busy that you are turning work away rather than struggling to find work and having to pay staff for doing nothing.

◆ As an employer you have certain legal duties and responsibilities for your staff. Make sure you're fully familiar with them and that anyone you do employ has a written contract of employment.

CHAPTER 8

The Gardening Calendar

This is all about planning your future.

A year in the gardening business

We now live in a world where seasons are often confused. No longer can we predict with any degree of certainty what fortunes the weather will bring in spring. Summer can often be reminiscent of winter, and autumn of summer. As gardeners we must learn to cope with snow in April, brilliant sunshine in February and grass growing late in November.

The weather

Often when gardeners in the south of the country are taking covers off lawn mowers preparing for their first cut of the season, elsewhere in the country others may still be sweeping snow from pathways and clearing storm damaged trees. With this in mind, the information in this chapter is given more as a guide than a definitive directive on what you should do and when you should do it. **You will need to tailor the material to suit your own business and the climatic conditions you find yourself operating under.**

Be flexible

If running a gardening business has taught me anything, it is that flexibility is a key ingredient in making a successful business.

> While few might imagine painting a garden fence in December, I have been asked to undertake this task on more than one occasion and have willingly obliged. Similarly, I have found myself being instructed not to undertake necessary repairs to a greenhouse as wildlife was already over-wintering there. Your expertise and knowledge is worthless if you cannot satisfy the needs of your clients. If my clients would rather see their greenhouse face certain destruction than make wildlife homeless then I can only applaud their unselfishness.

However, this should not stop you from making a follow-up entry in your diary for spring, to return and either repair or replace the greenhouse as need be.

Planning ahead

During the summer months retailers plan their Christmas sales campaign, buyers attend trade fairs and orders are placed for Christmas stock. For us, who will be spending our summer time outdoors working, it's difficult to imagine planning this far ahead. But to do so is not only sensible, but essential if you are to comfortably survive the winter months, often a time when homeowners do not contemplate spending money on their gardens.

> **Any business that hopes to survive must plan for its future. Running a gardening business is no different from that of the retailer.**

You must plan ahead if you are to remain in business and profitable. To ignore the season that is just around the corner is a dangerous mistake.

In this chapter I have divided each month into two distinct areas:

- what to do in the garden
- what to do in the business.

If you're only planning to work during the spring or summer months then obviously your needs will differ from those of the all-year round business. However, if your aim is to start your business in the spring, then you will need to start preparations in the winter. *It's far better that you find clients prior to starting than starting and then trying to find work.* Similarly if you're working all year round you'll need to plan your sales campaign well in advance of your targeted season.

January

Happy New Year!

If you've worked all summer and autumn now is as good as any time to have a break and get away from it all. Forget the business for a few days, a week or even longer and treat yourself to a holiday. When you return you'll be ready to start planning to make this your most profitable and successful year in business.

In the business

The most important thing you have to do this month is to make sure that you get your tax return to the Inland Revenue by 31 January, and that you pay any tax that is due. A penalty of £100 will automatically be charged for a late return.

Other things that you will need to look at:

◆ Time to revise your business plan and take stock of the past year.

◆ Budgets – look at the past year's performance on expenditure and identify where in your business you can make savings.

◆ Plan your spring sales campaign. Write to all of your clients and those whose business you didn't manage to secure and remind them that it's never too soon to start preparing the garden for spring. If necessary, offer incentives.

◆ Tools – get your lawn mower and the like serviced, blades replaced and ready for the spring.

◆ Trade catalogues. When the weather's too bad for working outside, time spent sourcing trade suppliers will be time well spent. If you're planning a home-based nursery, or looking to benefit from spin-offs, now is the time to source wholesalers. The extra income you generate from selling compost, lawn care products and the like during spring, summer and autumn will compensate for your loss of earnings during these months – but only if you put the work in now.

Services you can offer

Although January is generally considered a quiet month in the garden, there are still a number of jobs that need to be done, which include:

◆ Greenhouse repairs.
◆ Fencing erection and repairs.
◆ Gates, sheds and footpath maintenance.
◆ Frost protection service – wrapping up trees and plants in straw to protect from winter frosts.
◆ Winter digging – provided the ground is neither water-logged nor iced over, beds, borders and vegetable patches can be dug over.
◆ New lawns – sites can be prepared, and if weather permits turf can be laid.

- Weeding.
- Offer a service to supply and dig in compost.
- Ensure that all tree and shrub stakes are secure and will not suffer wind rock. This may mean replacing old stakes.
- Planting – bare-root trees and shrubs can be planted.
- Fruit tree pruning – apple and pear trees.
- Hedges – deciduous hedges can cut as well as planted.
- Lawns can be repaired and drainage problems rectified.
- Fruit trees can be sprayed.
- Christmas trees – now that no one wants them advertise a take away and dispose service.

February

February, the shortest month of the year, can be the harshest with strong winds, high rainfalls, frosts and heavy falls of snow. Difficult weather brings opportunities for your business with fencing being blown down, sheds overturned and greenhouse window panes sprayed like confetti over lawns and borders.

In the business

Get the tax man off your back! If as yet you haven't settled your tax bill, then in addition to interest payments a 5% surcharge will apply from 28 February on all tax that fell due on 31 January.

Continue planning your spring sales strategy. You could also take advantage of the dark evenings and spend your time reading and studying gardening manuals. Local agricultural colleges offer many worthwhile short courses.

If you're planning a lawn-cutting round make sure that you have all your advertisements in place. Depending on the climate you enjoy, or endure, next month may well be the start of the lawn-cutting season.

Services you can offer

- Winter digging, soil preparation for spring.
- Cutting back any overgrown shrubs and hedges.

- Fruit tree pruning.
- Fruit tree feeding (potash).
- Pruning roses – depending on weather, and if they have already been pruned prior to Christmas.
- Bare-rooted trees, shrubs and roses can be planted.
- Seasonal pruning of late-flowering shrubs such as buddleia, ceanothus and hardy fuchsias.
- Turfing.
- Fencing erection and repairs.
- Greenhouse repairs.
- Supply and dig in compost.

March

Spring is a magical time for gardeners everywhere. If this is your first year in this business, I imagine that you will be pleasantly surprised at the steady flow of clients asking for your help with their gardens. This is also the month when the clocks go forward so you can look forward to longer hours of daylight and increasing your workload. The downside is that March is renowned for its bitterly cold winds, which makes outdoor work difficult.

In the business

- Time to start planning your summer sales campaign.

- For those preparing to launch a gardening round now is the time to advertise your business. Get your cards up as soon as you possibly can this month and you can start earning almost straight away.

- If your business includes selling plants and shrubs now is the time to put the final touches to your catalogues, brochures or web site in preparation for taking orders.

- Garden coaching. Now is a good time to start advertising this service.

Services you can offer

- Lawn care – scarifying (for those clients who did not have it done in the autumn).

Repairing damaged lawns by either re-turfing or seeding.

◆ Lawn-cutting – time to start mowing regularly.

◆ New lawns – turfing and seeding new lawns.

◆ Soil preparation – digging over and preparing the soil for those clients who want to lay their own turf or seed.

◆ Planting summer flowering bulbs. The secret is to plant them at set intervals over the coming weeks, which will result in an ongoing floral display as opposed to everything happening at once.

◆ Hedges – last chance to plant bare-rooted hedges.

◆ Rose pruning.

◆ Lift and divide summer-flowering herbaceous perennials.

◆ Fruit trees – feed all with potash.

April

This is the month when your business will come alive as householders turn their attention to their gardens. Sales will be given a generous helping hand from Mother Nature whose unfolding beauty will now be apparent in those gardens that have been well looked after. Plants come alive after their winter hibernation and the wonderful aroma that is spring is all around us.

Gardens that have been neglected will now appear even more acutely in need of attention as a fresh new growth of weeds takes an even stronger hold, often making it impossible to navigate around pathways and driveways. This creates an opportunity for your skills and expertise. Don't forget to leaflet-drop such properties.

In the business

This is the month when you will receive your self-assessment forms from the Inland Revenue. It's a good idea to complete it when it arrives as opposed to storing it, forgetting about it until the day it suddenly becomes a terrible rush.

My aim during this and the coming months is to spend as little time as possible bogged down with paperwork and bookwork.

With spring well and truly here, you should now be looking to spend as much time as possible out there working.

Services you can offer

- Lawn-cutting.
- Lawn feeding.
- Turfing.
- Garden clearances.
- Hard feature erection service – greenhouses, pergolas.
- Pathway cleaning.
- Planting – evergreen trees and shrubs.
- Seasonal pruning.
- Dividing perennials.
- Cut down any dead growth left over after the winter.
- Spray roses.
- Pest control service – slug eradication service, using either organic methods or pellets.
- Deadheading daffodils and treating them to a feeding, which makes for better flower heads the following year.
- Hedges – plant evergreen hedges.
- Prepare beds and borders for bedding plants.
- Composting services.
- Ponds – cleaning service.

May

For those running gardening rounds you should now be actively working to fill your diary, that's if you haven't already reached this stage. Remember to include as many spin-offs as you possibly can. Your clients will want bedding plants, seeds, composts, lawn care products and a whole range of things. What better way to boost your earnings than supplying them yourself?

In the business

Don't forget to keep a close eye on your business affairs too.

♦ Spend a bit of time reading through your original business plan and assessing how your first week, month or quarter has gone.

♦ Are you achieving your sales targets? If not, then what do you need to do to achieve them?

♦ Expenditure – are you spending more or less than you'd anticipated? If you're exceeding your initial budgets and exceeding your initial sales figures then your figures may well balance each other out. But if you're spending more than you'd initially planned, you need to put the brakes on. If you're not careful costs can spiral at this time of the year as things get busier.

Services you can offer

♦ Lawn care – feeding and weed control.
♦ Lawn-cutting.
♦ Turfing.
♦ Clearing out spring bedding.
♦ Planting.
♦ Seasonal pruning.
♦ Garden clearance.
♦ Garden planning service.
♦ Garden makeovers.
♦ Pest control.
♦ Prune clematis after flowering.
♦ Staking service for tall plants.
♦ Greenhouse cleaning.
♦ Shed clearances.
♦ Fencing work.
♦ Painting and wood treatments of fences, sheds, summerhouses etc.

June

With the summer now well and truly arrived, all sorts of opportunities unfold. Gardening rounds should now be picking up momentum and soon be at a stage where there is no room left for new regular clients. If this is not the case then re-read Chapter 6.

In the business

Summer is a time for annual holidays, which provides enormous opportunities for offering a garden sitting service. This is a business that you can operate from now until the end of August and beyond if the weather permits. Nothing is worse than having taking two weeks' holidays only to return home to find that in your absence favourite plants have been scorched to death and your prized lawn is brown and burnt. *What could be better than leaving your garden in the capable hands of a professional gardener who will undertake all the necessary work, including watering, dead-heading etc in your absence?*

Advertising:

- This is a service than can be advertised in shop windows, magazines, newspapers and so on.

- The most effective place is local magazines and newsletters, or get some leaflets printed and convince your local travel agents to distribute them to holidaymakers.

- Another worthy place to advertise your service is at local boarding kennels and catteries, doctors' and dentists' surgeries.

Other services

- Lawn care.
- Pest control.
- Beds and borders care – weeding, deadheading etc.
- Seasonal pruning.
- Planting up containers and borders with seasonal bedding.
- Garden clearance.
- Garden makeovers.
- Garden coaching.
- Rose care – treating greenfly and removing suckers.

- Fencing work.
- Vegetable gardening.
- Lifting and dividing bulbs.
- Plant up and sell hanging baskets.

July

In the business

Gardening rounds and lawn-cutting operations will be in full swing this month with plenty of regular maintenance to be attended to. This is a time that many regular gardeners' diaries are full and therefore now is a good time for the newcomer to launch their business.

Tax due. The only thing this month to dampen your spirits is that your second payment on account to the Inland Revenue will be due at the end of the month. You should also, if you haven't already, give some thought to completing last year's tax return. If you would like the Inland Revenue to calculate your tax bill for you then you must send them your completed return before 30 September. Obviously the later you do this, the more time you will have to wait before finding out how much your tax liability is going to be. *My advice is to complete your form as early as possible. This way you can accurately budget for your tax liability in your forecasts.*

Services you can offer

- Garden sitting service for holidaymakers.
- Garden clearance.
- Hedge trimming.
- Lawn care and cutting.
- Seasonal pruning.
- Garden coaching.
- Wood treatment of fencing, summer houses, sheds etc.
- Planting seasonal bedding (last chance).
- Preparing ground for new lawns ready to be laid in the autumn.
- Rose care – deadheading and feeding.
- Prune wisteria.

◆ Fruit trees – thin out remaining fruit after June falls.

August

This is often the quietest month of the year. Gardeners with gardening rounds will find much of their work concerned with maintaining order and beauty in the garden as opposed to undertaking any heavy work. Lawn-cutting services will not be affected by any downturn in work, but the same cannot be said for those running general gardening businesses. It is here that the 'quiet' period will be felt most, but this should not impact too drastically on your sales provided you've been prudent and forward planned.

In the business

Next month you'll find your services in great demand as the autumn begins in earnest. If you've worked hard during the winter, moved mountains in the spring and had a busy summer so far, why not take a break and have a holiday? I shut my business completely for the latter two weeks of August and take a well-deserved holiday. Obviously, if you are operating either a gardening round or a lawn-cutting service, this will not apply to you. But for anyone else operating an all-year round gardening business, now is as good a time as any to take yourself off and recharge those batteries in anticipation of the autumn deluge!

But don't forget to:

◆ Review how your business has operated during the last months and identify the areas you need to improve on.

◆ Decide now whether or not you're going to keep your business open all year round. If you decide to keep your business open you will need to plan your autumn and winter sales strategy.

Services to offer

◆ Garden sitting service.
◆ Watering service.
◆ Beds and borders maintenance.

- Lawn-cutting.
- Seasonal pruning.
- Fruit trees – last opportunity to summer-prune apple and pear trees.
- Hedge trimming.
- Garden clearance.
- Rose care – deadheading.
- Preparing the soil for new lawns to be laid in the autumn.

September

All too quickly our summer is gone, evenings are getting shorter and we're heading towards that least favoured of times – winter. But don't despair. Autumn is one of the busiest times in the gardening year and certainly there is no shortage of work for you to be getting on with.

In the business

You have until 30 September to send your tax return to the Inland Revenue, should you wish them to calculate your tax liability for you. Otherwise you must send your tax return and pay your tax due on or before 31 January.

      If you're operating a gardening round or lawn-cutting service, and you are planning to close your business for the winter months, then September may well be your last month of trading. Whether or not you continue through October and November will depend on climatic conditions. My experience has been that regular clients are keen to have their gardens 'put to bed' by early October at the latest. Remember, too, that from now on the days will be getting shorter, which will result in you having less working hours available in your diary.

Services you can offer

- Pre-season greenhouse service. Now is the time to have broken window panels, leaks and uncooperative doors sorted out before the bad weather begins.

- Autumn garden clearance.

- Leaf sweeping and removal service – this is a very popular service. Few people enjoy having to wade through and sweep up seemingly unending piles of leaves.

◆ Planting time for new trees, shrubs.

◆ Transplanting time for many evergreen shrubs.

◆ Scarifying service. This involves removing dead grass, weeds and moss from the lawn's surface. Hiring a machine is usually more cost effective than purchasing one.

◆ Aeration service, reducing compacting on the lawn which has occurred during the summer period. Generally achieved by using a garden fork, but depending on the surface area of the lawn you may find that you need to hire a machine. Don't be tempted to buy one.

◆ Turfing. Ideal time to lay new turf.

◆ Cut down and divide perennials.

◆ Clean beds and borders of spent bedding plants and dig in some quality compost.

◆ Garden ponds – cover with netting to prevent leaves from covering the water.

◆ Seasonal pruning.

◆ Give hedges a final tidy-up.

October

Towards the end of October many seasonal or part-time gardening businesses will close. Lawn-cutting services will most likely have completed their final cut by the time the month draws to an end. General gardening businesses will still be very busy.

In the business

If you're shutting your business now is the time to finalise your accounts. Don't be tempted to put the books away promising to look at them again prior to re-starting, because there is no better time than the present to analyse your seasonal performance.

◆ Cast a critical eye over your expenditure and look at ways of reducing your costs and making your operation more efficient.

◆ Sales – did you achieve your seasonal targets? If you exceeded then great, now set even more ambitious ones for next year. But if you failed to meet them you'll need to know why. If this was your first season in business, then perhaps you were over-ambitious. Don't be too hard on yourself, but do look at ways of improving your performance and maximising profit.

◆ Services – now is as good a time as any to prune the list of services you offer. Get rid of those that you feel just weren't worth it, or that you particularly didn't enjoy doing.

◆ Prices – by the end of your first season you'll have a better idea of market rates in your area. How did your prices compare? If generally you found that your prices raised no objections, or that you didn't lose any work to a competitor, this indicates that you may have been undercharging.

Services to offer

◆ General gardening clearance.
◆ Leaf clearance.
◆ Pre-winter wind check. This is where you ensure that all stakings for trees and shrubs are secure and replace those that aren't.
◆ Hedge trimming where necessary.
◆ Digging service. Autumn is the best time for digging over soil and then leaving it for the winter frosts to break down.
◆ Turfing.
◆ Cutting back remaining perennials that have finished flowering.
◆ Continue where necessary lifting and dividing clumps of perennials.
◆ Fencing – repairs and erections.
◆ Seasonal pruning.

November

There is still lots to do this month clearing out gardens and preparing them for winter.

In the business

Depending on the weather you will find that you now have time for getting on with bookwork and business planning. Similar to those operating seasonal rounds, now is a good time to review past performances and work out future strategies.

Services to offer

- Garden clearances.
- Leaf clearance.
- Winter digging.
- Turfing.
- Greenhouse repairs.
- Fencing erection and repairs.
- Fruit trees – winter pruning.
- Hedge trimming – conifers.
- Planting – bare-rooted roses.
- Winter pruning of deciduous trees and shrubs can now begin.

December

Happy Christmas!
Cold and rain will now be an unwelcome visitor to your business. However, don't despair. Before you know it you'll be turning over a new year in your diary and looking forward to the spring.

In the business

There is still lots to do in the garden. My experience has been that the worse the weather the busier you will be. Make sure that you have adequate clothing to see you through this period. You'll need a good set of waterproofs (make sure you get a waterproof high visibility jacket for when you're working roadside) and some decent fleeces.

Services to offer

- Christmas trees. Quite rightly there is increasing interest in sustainable Christmas trees. You could put together a package, which includes supplying and fixing the Christmas tree indoors, returning in January to plant the tree outside.

◆ Garden clearance.

◆ Winter pruning.

◆ Rose pruning.

◆ Supplying and fitting greenhouse insulation.

◆ Removing unwanted shrubs.

◆ Winter digging.

◆ Composting.

Managing your diary

It's essential that when you are asked to do something that is not possible because it is not in season, for example laying a new lawn in August, you book the work in for a later date. For example:

◆ Start booking autumn scarification and aeration treatments in summer when you discuss lawn care with your clients.

◆ If you're asked to do some digging in the height of the summer when the ground is like concrete, book the work in for the autumn. Agree a price, book the work in your diary and confirm the appointment in writing.

If you adopt this strategy then difficult months become easier and you won't find that you wake up in the small hours of the morning worrying about having enough work to see you through the winter months.

> The most important tool you have is your diary. Make sure you use it. Remember there are 365 days in a year. So if you're booked out this week or month there are other times available. Never say that you are booked out. There is always time available!

Summary

- Get into the habit of forward planning. You should be planning your winter sales campaign in summer, your spring campaign in winter and so on.

- Be imaginative. Wet and windy conditions may mean that you can do little actual gardening, but there will be lots of fences to repair, greenhouses damaged and so on.

- Continually monitor your performance against your business plan and don't be afraid to revise and review your business goals.

- Use your diary – by far the best tool in your armoury. Make it work for you!

CHAPTER NINE

Avoiding Seasonal Blues

When things don't always go to plan

Despite your best efforts no business can ever run completely smoothly all of the time. There will be hitches and snags along the way, occasions when things don't go how you'd wish them to. Many of the undesirable eventualities that may befall your business can be predicted to a certain degree. By recognising these now and taking steps to ensure you don't unwittingly invite disaster into your life, you can take positive action to avoid them, thus saving your energies for those few circumstances that are completely out of your control. This chapter identifies some of these problems and highlights likely solutions, making your operation more disaster proof.

Gardening – a dangerous business

Every year gardeners both amateur and professional will climb unsafe ladders in the belief that an accident won't happen to them. Others will continue to use tools and equipment that are positively unsafe and dangerous. *Avoiding seasonal blues doesn't just mean staying safe, it means staying alive.* Gardening is a dangerous business. Nothing should be left to chance. Get it right and you'll enjoy running one of the most rewarding businesses in the world, but ignore your safety or that of others and you could end up paying for it with your life.

As well as physical dangers, there are psychological challenges. Research carried out into stressful occupations has discovered that the proprietors of small businesses, and self-employed people working from home, are likely to suffer more in the way of stress than if they were employees.

You may think that swapping a hectic working life dogged with commuting problems for your own gardening business would be a stress-buster, but possibly this will not be the case. Running your own business brings with it a whole new set of problems and challenges – the experience can either be enjoyable and fulfilling or highly stressful, perhaps even more so than the environment you left behind.

Before starting your business, look again at the reasons why you want to do this.

I started by business because I wanted more in the way of ndependence, fun and income.

- **Independence** – the freedom to be my own boss and break free from the limiting working environment I'd become accustomed to.
- **Fun** – I don't see why going to work has to be a struggle or something that cannot be enjoyed. When I started my business, I wanted to work at something that I knew I would enjoy.
- **Profit** – without it, I can't live the life I want to live. If you wish to remain in business for any length of time, your venture must be profitable. Having a profitable business means that you can enjoy the experience even more.

So what makes self-employment so stressful?

Imagine that you are leaving your present job with its stresses, strains and long hours to start your own home-based gardening business. You've fully researched your business idea and are confident that you can make it work. Your family is enthusiastically behind your plans and agree that it is time for you to go it alone. Financially you're relatively sound and have at least three months of survival income sitting in a high interest rate account, which hopefully won't be touched unless you really need it. Business planning is something that you have enjoyed doing and you worked out a clear launching strategy from which to work from to catapult your business into the market.

But this is only half of the picture. You're giving up much more than a job. What you're leaving is a way of life:

- The support and friendship of your colleagues.

- Either a wage or salary paid to you weekly or monthly.

- Paid leave.

- Depending on your employer you may have been paid while you were off sick.

- Bank holiday pay.

- Job security.

- When you leave work at the end of the day, you are physically removed from it, even if you take work home you have left your working environment, which in itself is refreshing.

♦ If things don't go well there are often other people or circumstances that can be blamed.

Being self-employed means that:

♦ Most of the time you will be working on your own.

♦ You will not have the 'family environment' of many work places to fall back on.

♦ You will have to accept responsibility for your business in terms of both its success and failures.

♦ Work isn't over when you've completed your last job of the day. When you get home there will be telephone calls to return, bookwork, quotations and preparing for the next day.

♦ Taking a day off either through illness or holiday means loss of earnings.

♦ Factors outside of your business can have a negative impact on your earnings, bad weather being the most common offender.

♦ Your working environment is where you live. Separating home and working life can often be difficult.

All of these things can make life more stressful and less enjoyable. Therefore it's essential that prior to starting your business you really do believe that this is for you. It would be far better for you now to realise that this really isn't for you as opposed to adopting the attitude that you'll give it a try and see how it goes. I can tell you now that unless you're prepared to give yourself 100% to your business, then things won't go very well.

> **If you're going to start this business, then make sure that you are ready for the hard work ahead. This doesn't make it any less enjoyable, if anything it makes it far more worthwhile.**

Factors outside your control

There will be times when your plans are thwarted by factors outside your control such as:

◆ weather
◆ machinery breakdowns
◆ health and well-being
◆ family/personal problems.

However, there are certain things that you can do to reduce your exposure to risks.

Weather

Weather is one of those factors which is completely out of your control but, as the next story demonstrates, you can still safeguard your investment and limit your loss.

I was just putting the finishing touches to a complete garden makeover. It had been a large job, which had taken almost two months to bring to the final stages. All that remained was to lay the turf. The soil had been prepared, but because the weather forecasters were predicting torrential rain for the following week, I was reluctant to order the turf.

My client was becoming impatient. The sooner the turf was down, the better as far as she was concerned. When I mentioned my concerns regarding the weather forecast, she dismissed this entirely. 'Surely a bit of rain won't do any harm?' she said.

But as anyone who has been unfortunate enough to have to lay turf in the rain will know, rarely is it successful. Depending on the severity of the rain, you could find yourself having to relay the whole lawn. Naturally, was this to happen it would have to be at my expense, so I was reluctant to take any chances.

Before making a final decision, I decided to check the forecast again. There had been no improvement, if anything the outlook had worsened. Vast quantities of rain were predicted to fall round about the same time as my turf was due to arrive. There was nothing for it but to put the job off. When I told my client that I would return three weeks later to lay the turf, provided of course the weather had improved sufficiently, she was disappointed. So was I. For I couldn't submit my final invoice until the garden was complete, which meant having to wait at least another three weeks before being paid. This meant that I now had almost £3,000 worth of materials tied up in a job that I still hadn't received any payment for.

The forecasters had got it right. As predicted it rained and rained until everywhere was flooded. Fire crews were travelling around in inflatable dinghies. An acquaintance of ours whose builder either hadn't bothered to check the forecast, or had decided to ignore it, watched helplessly as the new patio he had been laying was washed away to the bottom of the garden.

A group of landscapers who'd been laying turf at a new housing development ended up having to rip up and dispose of all the turfs they'd been laying. Thousands of pounds wasted in terms of materials and labour.

When the weather improved, I returned and laid the new lawn, which looked splendid against the backdrop of a whole new and exciting garden. My client was delighted with the end result as was I. Deciding not to go ahead with the turfing had been difficult. My client's insistence that everything would be OK, together with my own desire to finish the garden, get paid, and move on, hadn't made things easy. But in the end I was glad that I stuck to my gut feelings.

Expect the unexpected

Be prepared for anything. Although weather is something that is ultimately out of your control, checking weather forecasts and making informed decisions is something that you will have to do regularly. If things go wrong, as sometimes they will, you and you alone are responsible. Whether or not it is the fault of someone else is immaterial. The buck stops with you.

> **Make your own decisions. Take control of your business and do not let anyone else dictate to you how you run your operation. No one knows your business like you do.**

Machinery breakdowns

There are a few dos and don'ts when it comes to taking care of your machinery:

◆ Make sure that you have your equipment regularly serviced by someone who is suitably qualified.

◆ Familiarise yourself with the manufacturer's handbook for all your tools and make sure you are using the equipment correctly.

◆ Clean your equipment after every job, or if this is not feasible at the end of every day.

◆ Regularly check that all bolts, screws etc are tightened in accordance with the manufacturer's guidelines.

◆ Use the correct fuel mixtures.

◆ Look after your equipment and it will look after you.

Health and wellbeing

Since starting the business I have suffered less from the common ailments such as flu and the like that I suffered when I was an employee. Working outside in all weathers hasn't made me susceptible to colds and flu as much as I thought it would. I have felt much better for having left the environs of a large, open-plan office where it seemed there was always someone with a cold, tummy upset or whatever.

Nevertheless, you must look after your health, as without it you have nothing. Some things that I would recommend you do:

◆ **If you have any health problems** you should consult your doctor and ask for their advice prior to starting your business.

◆ **Drink at least eight glasses of water every day.** Dehydration is a killer.

◆ **Be careful how much tea and coffee** you drink.

◆ **Always have a good, healthy breakfast** before going to work and avoid traditional fry-ups.

◆ **Make sure you take regular breaks** during your working day and get a good night's sleep.

◆ **Never work machinery** when you're tired.

◆ **Avoid alcohol** during your working day.

◆ **Gardening involves lots of lifting** of heavy items; make sure that you know how to lift things correctly reducing likely damage to your back.

- **Always wear gloves.** I often wear two pairs, light comfortable ones underneath a pair of quality heavy-duty rubber gloves. As you'll soon discover, all sorts of nasty surprises lurk behind trees and bushes. I come across used hypodermic syringes, dead animals, vomit, human excrement and broken glass. Remember too that certain plants are toxic and should be handled with care, these include: amaryllis, chrysanthemums, cyclamen and poinsettias, just to name a few of those more frequently found.

- **First aid kit.** You should always have a comprehensive first aid kit with you at all times. Make sure your kit includes an eye bath and eye drops.

- **Always wear protective clothing** as appropriate to the job you are doing. I now wear protective eye glasses as a matter of course, as a friend of mine suffered a nasty eye injury as a result of a fairly minor accident. Gardens are full of things that swing back and slap you in the face when you're not expecting it. Then when you're on your knees busy weeding, it's easy to miss the rose bush hidden in the foliage.

- **Ladders.** Make sure that you invest in a quality set of ladders and that you use them in accordance with the manufacturer's safety instructions.

- **High visibility jacket.** Essential if you are doing any work on either the footpath or road. Make sure that any oncoming traffic can see you. If necessary place a warning triangle on the road or pavement.

- **Weed killers,** pesticides etc. Do not use them unless you are suitably qualified to do so. You must be trained in the correct use of any of these substances before using them on anyone's garden. Courses are usually run by your local agricultural college.

- **Instruction manuals**. Read all manufacturers' instruction manuals before operating any machinery.

- **Make sure that you are suitably trained** in the safe use of all the equipment you use. There are lots of courses you can undertake. Check with your local agricultural college for details. Time training is time well spent.

Family/personal problems

Hopefully, the occasions when you have either family or personal problems will be far and few between, but they do happen.

When a much-loved relative of mine died suddenly, I had no option but to close my business so that I could return to Ireland for the funeral and spend some time with my family. There was no one that I could hand my business over to, and at the time, as always, I had a full diary.

Fortunately, all of my clients were most understanding when I phoned to cancel their appointment. Nevertheless, I faced a near impossible situation when I returned to work as I was now effectively two weeks behind. Somehow, I managed to work my way through the backlog and see daylight again only managing to lose one client in the process.

The lesson I learnt was that there will be times that you will have to call for outside help.

By making a provision for these times now, prior to starting, you can ensure that if the worst happens and you have to leave your business unexpectedly then you can hand the reins over to someone else. If during this period you lose clients, don't despair. All is not lost. You can catch up. The most important thing is that while dealing with whatever crisis, bereavement, illness or other misfortune you find yourself coping, you have someone on whom you can rely on to answer your phone in your absence, or phone your clients to cancel appointments.

As soon as you return to your business after an sudden or unexpected period of leave, make sure that you:

◆ Contact all of those clients whose appointments you have had to cancel and explain and apologise for what happened.

◆ Re-plan your diary and work additional hours if necessary to catch up.

I've read of situations where people have lost their businesses through personal crisis. These things do happen, but remember that they can happen to you just as easily if you are an employee. Most employers will only give compassionate leave under certain circumstances, and often it falls to the employee to take time off at their own expense.

> **Make sure that you have someone reliable lined up to help you in the event of crisis. Even if their role is only to cover your phones, or phone your clients to rearrange an appointment, this can be invaluable.**

Difficult people and situations

Identifying the troublemakers

Let's face it, not everyone you work for will be amenable. Some will be downright rude. Others will complain regardless of what you do for them. They will constantly berate you for overcharging, and waste your time and energy with their incessant whingeing. *This latter group, the troublemakers, pose a serious threat to your business and you must do everything you possibly can to avoid them.* Not only if allowed will they destroy your confidence, but also make you unnecessarily wary of everyone else. Pretty soon you'll find that you'll be adopting a 'trust no one' philosophy, which is not helpful when you're trying to build a business.

I'm unable to give you a sure-fire way of recognising potential troublemakers, but in my opinion potential clients who demonstrate the following characteristics should either be treated with caution or avoided at all costs.

◆ Argumentative to the point of being offensive about how much you're proposing to charge them.

◆ Start listing all the gardeners they've had over the past few months, years etc, telling you how useless they all were and expressing doubt that you'll be any better.

◆ Promises of lots of future work provided you do today's job for next to nothing.

◆ Are downright unpleasant and nasty when you visit them.

The good news is that these people are very much in a minority. Most people who hire a gardener or landscaper do so with the very best intentions, and will be most agreeable provided of course your work is up to standard and you treat them with respect. But they do exist. You may attract more of these people when you start because they have such bad reputations amongst other tradespersons they cannot find anyone else willing to work for them, which means being constantly on the lookout for newcomers.

My strategy for dealing with these people is as follows:

◆ If you find yourself in a potential client's garden haggling over the price, or being accused of 'daylight robbery', then politely walk away.

♦ Under no circumstances argue with them, or anyone for that matter. You're a professional. People like these love nothing better than an argument.

♦ There's nothing wrong with deciding that you don't want to work for someone. Usually it's only when you get to meet the person for the first time that you can make any sort of informed decision. If you don't like what you see, or your gut instinct tells you this will be more trouble than it's worth, then walk way. Either tell them that you cannot do what they're asking or that you're too busy. But whatever you do, don't leave them under the impression that you'll get back to them with a price. Not only is this unprofessional, but it will lead to all sorts of problems with never-ending telephone correspondence.

Handling complaints

At some point you will receive a complaint from someone. I say someone, because often the person who will make a complaint is not actually your client, but a third party.

♦ This could be a neighbour annoyed because your van is parked on the road outside his property and not the property you're working at.

♦ A complaint because someone felt that you've either taken too much or too little off a boundary hedge.

♦ A passer-by irate that you haven't yet swept up the hedge trimmings, despite the fact that you have only just begun cutting.

♦ Someone complaining about the noise of your equipment. This is not as uncommon as you'd think. Lots of people work night duty, and as someone who has done so in the past, there is nothing worse than being woken up in the middle of a much-needed sleep by the buzzing of a strimmer, hedge trimmer or chainsaw.

Positive action

The way you handle all complainers is vital to your overall success. If you manage to annoy everyone in the neighbourhood, it's a fair bet that you won't be invited to return to do anyone else's garden. There's also the stress factor. Nothing is worse than having to work in an unhappy environment.

If you find that you are the subject of a number of complaints from the clients you are working at, you must listen to what they're telling you:

◆ Are they all complaining about the same thing?

◆ You must find ways of resolving things. This can only be achieved by actively listening to what they're telling you.

> **Try not to get all huffy and defensive when someone, whether your client or another person, complains. Listen to what they've got to say and try to put it right, there and then if you can.**

One afternoon I was sitting on the top of a tall conifer hedge, clipping the tops, when a voice from below bellowed: 'Oi, you son, what do you think you're doing?'

I looked down to find an elderly man standing in the middle of the pavement waving his stick up at me.

'What do you think you're doing?' he roared again.

Resisting the temptation to be unpleasant, I pointed out the obvious and told him that I was cutting the tops of the conifer hedging as I'd been instructed to do by the owner.

'And what are you going to do about these?' He shouted, scattering a bunch of clippings with his walking stick. When I told him that I'd be sweeping them up in due course, he wasn't satisfied.

'That's not much good to me now,' he shouted back. 'I could have fallen and injured myself on these while you're up there in the clouds not caring. I'd be suing you y'know. '

Anxious to avoid any unnecessary confrontation and spontaneous litigation action, I climbed down from the trees, and in an effort to pacify him, began sweeping up the clippings, even though I knew more would fall on exactly the same area once I resumed cutting. However, it did the trick. He was appeased, told me what a lovely job I was doing to the trees and how happy he'd be for me to come and do his, which wasn't exactly the invite I was hoping for.

Lessons learnt

While this man's initial approach had done little for my temper, I managed not to lose my cool. Rather than concentrate on him and his attitude, I concentrated on what he was telling me. His message was clear:

- The pavement was in a dangerous state as a result of my clippings and branches lying everywhere.

- Were someone to have injured themselves, either by being hit by a falling branch or tripping on the foliage, I was responsible.

- We're living in an increasingly litigious society where law firms actively encourage anyone who has so much has snubbed a toe on the pavement to sue for compensation. Unwittingly, I was leaving myself open to being sued.

I thanked him for his input. Now whenever I'm cutting a hedge that is likely to fall onto the pavement, I put up warning signs and sweep up regularly as I go. This is what being professional is all about.

Don't be offended by complaints. Often there is a valuable lesson to be learnt. Heed it, and you will most probably save yourself a lot of hassle in the future, ignore it and you invite untold misfortune.

One of the most common causes of complaint is that you have either misinterpreted your client's instructions or they have misunderstood what it is you said you would do.
     It is therefore vital that prior to starting a job you:

- Discuss fully and be as specific as you can about what you are going to do.

- When cutting hedges make sure you agree the exact height you will cut them down to. Nothing is more frustrating than, having spent a morning trimming a hedge you're then told that you didn't cut it down enough.

- Don't cut down or remove any trees until you check first that you are legally allowed to. In many situations you will need to apply for planning permission first. If you're the one who has cut something down, you're the one who will be held liable. I've mentioned before that tree work is best left to suitably qualified tree surgeons. There are good reasons for this.

- Discuss with your client the impact the work might have on neighbours. Often you will need the co-operation of the neighbouring property if you are to trim a boundary hedge successfully, or complete some job that entails you visiting their property. Putting up fencing is one such job where it's highly likely that you will have to stand in someone else's garden. Make sure you have their permission before starting.

Some guidelines for handling complaints:

- Listen to what the person is telling you.

- Don't interrupt them until they have finished.

- Try to resolve the complaint immediately, even if this means interrupting what you're doing.

- The word sorry can go a long way. Don't be afraid to use it as often as you need to.

- No matter how frivolous or even mischievous the complaint appears, losing your cool and entering into an argument won't solve anything. Simply put whatever it is right if you can and, if you can't, explain this to the complainant and then get on with whatever you were doing.

- When faced with a seemingly impossible complaint to resolve, tell the complainant that you will need their complaint in writing before responding further.

- If someone says that they intend taking legal action against you, request they put their complaint in writing. When you receive it, seek legal advice.

Complaints involving threats of legal action

No matter how frivolous and ridiculous the complaint may appear, if it is written by a solicitor on behalf of their client there are a number of things you should do straight away:

- Inform your insurance company and ask for their advice.

- You may find that within your business-banking package that you have access to free legal advice, if so this should be your first port of call.

- If you don't have a solicitor, and your insurance company recommends that you contact one, find a law firm that handles business matters.

Complaints can be expensive and time-consuming if not handled properly. Most complaints can be remedied immediately, provided you are willing to put yourself out. I strongly recommend that you do. A little time invested initially in bringing about a resolution can save enormous time, money and wasted energy in the future.

Motivation – keeping going

There is nothing more satisfying than breaking free from the past and leaving unhappiness behind. When you've reached this point and your business is up and running, you will need further goals and objectives to keep yourself going.

Good days and bad days

When your diary is full of work and you are working outdoors in brilliant sunshine with light cooling winds, energy levels are high, you are overflowing with enthusiasm and nothing will stop you from succeeding. But when there is more rain than sun, expenditure exceeds income and you feel you can no longer cope, this is the time when you owe it to yourself to continue with your venture at all costs.

When you can't see the future

When I'm not gardening or working in the business, I like nothing more than to sail. Sailing is one of those pastimes where from the moment you arrive at your boat, to the time you disembark you are consumed with what you are doing.

There are tides to plan for, charts to navigate, seas to negotiate, instruments to check, bearings to take, sails to raise, trim, lower, adjust and often all this during abysmal weather and terrible seas. Non-sailors cannot imagine why anyone would want to spend their leisure time engaged in such wet and cold activities. But for those bitten by the sailing bug, no explanation is needed.

Rough seas are usually accompanied by bad weather, which makes everything difficult. Navigation can become a stomach-churning affair as you struggle to read a chart whilst being knocked about unmercifully. It is during these times that fair-weather sailors decide it's not for them, when they can no longer enjoy calm waters and the reassuring sight of land they give up, return to shore and sell their boat. Dream over.

And so it is with many businesses that are run by their fair-weather proprietors who crave certainty.

Ten steps towards keeping your business on track:

1. Make sure you have a good business plan in place prior to starting.

2. If this is not the case, either revise the one you have, or write another.

3. Have a clear set of business and personal objectives.

4. Avoid negative people at all costs. Lots of people will enjoy nothing more than encouraging you to give up what you're doing. Consciously make efforts to avoid them.

5. Be your own best friend.

6. You are what you think – negative thinking is a destructive habit. Work every day on building a positive frame of mind.

7. If you can't work during periods of particularly bad weather, then make sure you enjoy your time off.

8. Always keep control of your business.

9. When things are most difficult, you must keep going. In the words of that famous song – don't give up until it's over.

10. Nothing is impossible – only difficult.

Your business plan

Use your business plan to pull you through any difficult times. Make sure that your plan includes your vision of a successful business and a successful self. If things are getting you down, reading positive images will pick you up.

♦ Work to achievable goals and targets.
♦ Nothing will frustrate you more than working to unachievable goals and deadlines.

Success means different things to different people. Your business plan must include a clear vision of what you're hoping to achieve. This could mean working less hours so that you can spend more time with your family or a hobby, or perhaps another business. Or it could mean working as many hours as you possibly can to earn enough to repay a debt, save for the holiday of a lifetime, or whatever.

The important thing is that you outline this vision in your business plan. Then when things get tough and the going seems to be all uphill, you can revisit your plan and remember why you're doing what you're doing.

Case study

Gill works as a customer services agent for mobile telephone company in a large call centre. She works five days a week, from 4pm to midnight, Sunday to Thursday. The unsocial hours mean that she has can only spend two evenings a week with her two young children. She often has difficulty sleeping, as there is no time for her to relax between finishing work and going to bed. When and if she does finally does get any sleep she is woken by the children, excited their mother is now home. The whole experience has left her tired and irritable. She realises that she cannot keep going as she is.

Gill discusses setting up her own gardening business with her husband Matt, who shares her enthusiasm. They both work out a business plan. Gill writes her 'vision' for her business. In it she highlights that her main reason for starting the business is that she can spend more quality time with her children without suffering any loss of earnings.

Gill has two motivating factors for starting her own business:

◆ Spend more time with her children.
◆ Earn sufficient to cover the loss of earnings caused by giving up her regular job.

These are two powerful objectives, which Gill has written into her plan. If she visits her business plan regularly, and particularly during any time she finds difficulty in continuing, she will be given some powerful reminders of why she started her business.

Self-motivation is crucial to your success. You cannot rely on either your clients, or even those closest for you, to do it for you. This is something that only you can do. Identify clearly why it is you're starting your business. Be specific with your needs:

◆ I need to have more freedom
◆ I need to earn more
◆ I want a better way of life.

The 40-hour a week myth

I've never understood why we're conditioned to work 40 hours a week. I believe that if company bosses told their work force that they could have every Monday off provided their work didn't suffer, in the vast majority of cases work output would remain the same, if not enhanced. Obviously it wouldn't work for every business or service, but I believe the majority of us could complete what we're doing in four days as opposed to the mandatory five.

There is no rule that says you must garden 40 hours a week if you are to be successful. What your financial expectations are will determine how much time you will spend working. So don't be afraid to work a four-day week if you can afford to do so. Just think what you can do with the rest of your time. *The very nature of gardening as a business makes it ideal for both part-time or full-time operation. Choose whatever suits you.*

Building your knowledge

Knowledge is confidence

One of the things that I most dreaded when I began was being asked to identify a shrub or plant that I didn't recognise. This fear was well founded. Often, during initial visits to new clients, I would be asked what so and so shrub or bush was. Despite my best efforts, I wouldn't be able to identify whatever it was and I'd have to say what I dreaded most: 'I don't know'. It was during these times that my confidence took a knock. My thoughts were who would employ anyone to tend to their garden when it was obvious they didn't know the names of all the plants and shrubs? But I was wrong.

You don't have to know the names of everything to be a good gardener, but it helps if you know the common ones.

It is neither possible nor expected that you will always be able to identify every plant, shrub or tree that you are asked about. However, you must be able to recognise, and have sufficient plant care knowledge, of all the common garden plants and shrubs and be able to distinguish between an annual and a perennial.

If your knowledge is lacking, don't despair. There are a number of ways that you can learn more.

Your local garden centre and nurseries

Taking regular walks around your local nurseries and garden centres will pay huge dividends. Look at all the plants. See how they are laid out in the sales areas. What plants form part of the herbaceous border display? What plants are recommended for shady spots? Look carefully at what people are buying. Is there a common theme? You'll soon find that there is. *The vast majority of visitors will buy much the same selection of bedding plants, herbaceous plants and the like.* Undertake regular visits and don't forget to ask the garden centre staff for advice and help. Ask them what their best sellers are and what would they recommend for a shady spot, sunny spot and so on. It's all useful information – **knowledge is confidence.**

Part-time job

If your knowledge is really lacking you could consider taking a part-time job at your local garden centre or nursery. You will quickly pick things up and get to know all the shrubs and plants, their likes and dislikes. You'd also be in an ideal position to find clients!

Seed and plant catalogues

These are great for highlighting both the seasonal favourites and new plants and shrubs on sale. If you don't already have any, the easiest and quickest way of acquiring them is to buy a gardening magazine and check the classifieds for companies that offer mail order. You can order vast quantities of catalogues, either by phoning up and requesting them or ordering them online. All of the major mail order companies now have their own web sites.

Books and magazines

As well as being able to recognise and correctly identify plants and shrubs, you will need to have a good knowledge of what's involved in caring for them. It's no good being able to recognise forsythia, for example, if you don't know when and how to prune it. There are many good books on the market ranging from encyclopaedias to pocket guides. I favour both – good quality encyclopaedias for my home office and pocket guides for my van.

Television programmes

Gardener's World is still my favourite, for rather than encouraging us to cover our slices of earth with concrete, bark and shingle and paint our fences purples, this programme is still primarily concerned with how and why things grow. Find the time to watch it regularly if you can and if the time is unsuitable record it.

It's a good idea to keep abreast of all gardening programmes. You'll find that many of your potential clients will be inspired to phone you after watching them. Often their questions will be more related to what they saw on the television than what is in their garden. I've lost count of the times that I've been asked: 'What was that big, lovely, purple, no it wasn't purple... a sort of blue plant they had on the telly last night?'

The internet

This can be a very useful reference tool. There is an explosion of gardening web sites on the internet, where you can find all sorts of specialist information concerning plant care. Amateur enthusiasts maintain many of these sites and the quality of the content can vary considerably. The good ones are invaluable reference tools providing pictures and information on every plant imaginable. I have found that there are a number of sites now devoted to individual plants. There are hosta web sites, rose care web sites, climbing rose web sites and so on.

Courses

There are a number of colleges now offering correspondence courses on all sorts of gardening subjects. You'll find a number of them listed in the help directory. Many of them include a syllabus for formal qualifications. *Why not study while you run your business? This is a great way of building up your theoretical knowledge and having a tutor to call on to answer all your questions.*

Your local horticultural college will almost certainly run short courses throughout the year.

Your clients

Many of my clients are keen gardeners but have come to that stage in their lives when they can no longer cope with the physical demands of their gardens. I have learnt so much from listening to these people, all of whom have been willing to share their knowledge and expertise. If any of your clients are keen gardeners don't be afraid to ask them for advice and information. You never know what you might learn.

Invest the time and money needed to perfect your craft. The difference between a good and a bad gardener is that one knows what they are doing and the other doesn't.

Nothing beats arriving to quote for a gardening job confident that your knowledge and expertise are up to whatever you're being asked. This is somewhat of a rarity in this business.

Successful Selling

Getting the business. So you've written your business plan, identified your niche, worked out a pricing structure, marketed your services, managed to get your telephone to ring, now all you have to do is visit your prospective clients and sell yourself to them. Simple as that, or is it?

Getting a foot in the door

By their nature, professional gardeners tend to be a quiet lot, shy, even. Of the professional gardeners that I have spoken to while researching this book, most readily admit that they would rather be weeding a difficult 50-foot border than having to find new clients, which is why many opt for the relative comfort of a gardening round. *For you to see your business grow into something more than just another job, you must be not only able to sell, but willing to sell. Unless you adopt an enthusiastic approach to selling, all your hard work and investment to date will be wasted.*

What are you afraid of?

Try to identify what it is you don't like about selling. Having identified the reason or reasons, work on eliminating them. Some of your reasons could include:

◆ meeting people for the first time
◆ telling them how much the job is likely to cost
◆ not being able to answer all of their questions
◆ lack of confidence.

Meeting people for the first time

If you're nervous about meeting people for the first time there are a number of positive steps that you can take to improve your confidence and make sure your meeting goes smoothly.

- Create a positive image in your mind of how you see your meeting going. If you keep seeing yourself as being confident and positive then you will find that's how you'll be. Work on the positive you!

- Always allow yourself sufficient time to get to your given appointment.

- Don't book specific times. Instead, say you'll be there between 2 and 2.30 depending on traffic. Nothing is worse than arriving at an appointment either too early or too late, so give yourself a half-hour window in which to arrive.

- During the initial telephone conversation with your client, make sure you ask enough questions to allow yourself to research the forthcoming job. For example, if you're being asked to come and prune some shrubs ask what they are. If your client doesn't know their names then don't worry. But if they do, at least you have an opportunity to read up on their pruning regime.

- Dress comfortably and appropriately. Prospective clients will not be expecting to see you arrive in a suit and tie. That said, neither would they be expecting you to be dressed as if you were heading off to a football match or the beach. Dressing appropriately will not only increase your confidence but help towards creating the right overall impression, which can only help the selling process.

- If you're going to be late, make sure you phone in advance to advise your client.

- During the meeting – listen more than you talk! This alone will make you appear more confident and professional.

Telling them how much it's going to cost

Your initial meeting has gone well. The prospective client has identified all they want done. It's a good job; you're keen to get it. Then they say those awful words: 'How much is it going to cost?'

It's a straightforward job to price. No outside materials are needed. Your calculations only need to include labour, tipping fees and an element of profit. Your client is waiting for an answer. You have two choices:

- give them an estimate there and then
- send them a written estimate at some time in the future.

**If you know how much the job is going to cost,
you should give your price during the initial meeting.**

The only time you should provide a written estimate of your charges, without first discussing them with your prospective client, is when you have to include additional costs that require researching. Certainly it is good practice to send a written confirmation of all your estimates, including those that you have already agreed.

The reason it is so important to price your job immediately is:

◆ People like to know how much things are going to cost without having to wait days for written estimates. By giving an immediate price, you either get a yes or a no. If you get a yes, and there is no reason why this shouldn't be the case, then agree a provisional date to start the work and make an entry in your diary. Follow this up with a written confirmation.

◆ If when you give your price your client says that you are too expensive, you can ask why, thus giving you an opportunity to overcome their objections there and then. There may be a number of reasons why you won't be given the job. Some people simply won't have imagined how much the job was going to cost, and now realise they cannot afford it. Alternatively, they may have had a cheaper estimate from a competitor. Or, as is more often the case, they intend to phone up that advertisement that says: 'We'll beat any price.'

◆ Your prospective client may have arranged for another company to provide an estimate and they may be attending later the same day. They may give their order to them solely on the basis that your competitor has been able to give them an immediate price and an indication, or date, as to when they can do the job, something which you have been unable to do.

Don't shy away from discussing your prices. You are operating a business, not a charity, and no one should expect you to work for nothing. Of course there may be some who do, *but the vast majority of your clients will expect a fair price for a good job.*

Overcoming objections

Objections are the reasons that people give you for not using you. For example, you're too expensive, or they know someone who can do it cheaper, and so on.

You should not see any objection as being finite. If someone says that you're too expensive that doesn't necessarily mean that they're not going to ask you do the job.

> I pride myself on being known locally as 'expensive, but very good', because what this really means is that I'm offering value for money.

Many clients have already experienced the 'we'll beat any price' lot and are well aware that if you want a good job you have to pay for it.

> You have just spent a half-hour walking around Mrs Robinson's overgrown garden with her. She's told you that she wants all her hedges trimmed, borders weeded, and identified a number of large bushes that she wants removed. You estimate that it will take you two days to do the job. It's a heavy job and will involve lots of backbreaking digging, cutting and tidying. You'll need to include about £30 to cover the dumping fees. Your total estimate is for £230. When you tell Mrs Robinson this she says that it is too expensive.

Would you simply say OK and then leave? Or would you ask her why she feels that you are too expensive?

Obviously having spent a half-hour of your time with Mrs Robinson, and the cost of your travelling time to and from the appointment, it would be ludicrous for you to simply accept that you're too expensive, bid her good day and leave. *You need to overcome Mrs Robinson's objections.* To do this you first need to identify what they are:

◆ When someone gives you any objection make sure that you qualify it.

◆ If you are told that you are too expensive, ask them in relation to what or whom. Is it that they believe they can get the job done cheaper by another gardener?

◆ Have they underestimated how much the whole job is likely to cost?

> **You can only successfully overcome an objection if you know what it is.**
> **You must qualify every objection and make sure that you are clear as to the real reasons your client is not willing to give you the order.**

When overcoming price objections always offer alternatives without reducing your prices.

When Mrs Robinson tells you that you are too expensive there are a number of things that you can do without reducing the price. The way to do this is to suggest a number of alternatives:

- If she takes the clippings and debris to the dump it would be cheaper.

- Offer to do one day as opposed to two. Point out how much you could achieve in a day's clear-out and then at a later date you could return to clear the second half.

> **While price is a deciding factor in whether or not people will employ you, it is not the only one.**

Prospective clients will base their decisions on a number of factors:

- Are you professional?
- Do you come across as someone who knows what they're doing?
- Do they like you?
- Would they feel comfortable with you working in their garden?

Whatever you do, make sure that you do not reduce your price simply on the basis that you're too expensive. Remember being professional means not only working to professional standards but also charging a fair and honest price for your work.

If your price is too expensive in relation to another quote, or your prospective client believes that they can get cheaper elsewhere, then:

- Don't knock the competition. Don't relate any horror stories, real or imagined about your competitors. Not only is this unprofessional, but you'll ensure that you'll never get the order.

- Do make sure that you are quoting 'like for like'. Does the cheaper quote include dumping fees, clearing up afterwards, removing all the shrubs that your does?

- Do point out that you are insured. You should always have a copy of your insurance certificate with you when quoting and also include a copy with every written quote you send.

- Do break down your estimate with your client, showing how and why you have arrived at the price you have.

◆ If you don't get the order, make sure that you leave on good terms and thank your prospective client for asking you to quote. Leaving in a huff and slamming the gate will only reinforce in your client's mind that they made the right decision by not hiring you.

◆ Don't be surprised if at a later date you get a telephone call asking you to do the job. The next person to walk through their gate and give a quote may be the gardener from hell. They do exist.

THE GOLDEN RULE OF SELLING

When you have given your price – *shut up*. Say absolutely nothing. Even if the silence is unbearable, do not be the first one to speak. You'll be surprised at the end of what might appear to be an unnatural silence, your client will say – OK, when can you do it?

It's easy when faced with a long silence to break it. At the time nothing seems worse than standing with your prospective client waiting for them to say anything. But wait you must, for if you interrupt too soon you will disrupt the selling process. *What may seem like an eternity to you is in reality only the few seconds it takes your client to decide whether or not to say yes.*

Don't forget to ask for the order

Whenever you give a quote or an estimate, either verbally or in writing, always ask for the business. Use your diary. Open it and say: 'Well Mrs Robinson, I could do the job for you a week on Friday, would that be convenient?'

If you think this is too pushy, don't. You're the one who has invested their time and money in visiting. The least you should do when you get there is ask for the job.

Selling for garden designers and landscapers

If your business involves creating and building a new garden you face a number of competitors:

◆ other designers and landscapers
◆ travel agents
◆ interior decorating companies

◆ home appliance companies
◆ your client – doing it themselves.

In an earlier chapter I mentioned that my most fearsome competitor is the travel agent. Usually people have to make a choice between having a new garden, going on a good holiday, having a new kitchen or conservatory or getting the entire house double-glazed. Only occasionally (once in my experience) will you find that people will have all of these things at the one time.

Always remember these unseen and often unmentioned competitors that are also vying for your client's disposal income. The companies that sell these things have invested thousands of pounds in marketing their products, strategies that are designed to make your client want to move out of their cold, wet and miserable garden and into a new kitchen, tropical conservatory or fly them off to foreign shores.

You'll have to be equally resourceful in promoting your business.

◆ Whenever you undertake to create a new garden make sure that you photograph your work. Before and after pictures make great selling tools on future jobs.

◆ Consider having your own web site where you can load pictures of your designs and work.

◆ Have attractive advertising signboards placed outside the property you are working at.

◆ Leaflet-drop the all the houses in the neighbourhood where you are working.

When selling against holidays and the like remember to sell the benefits of having a new garden:

◆ Enhance the value of the property.
◆ Makes the property more saleable and desirable.
◆ Safe place for the children to play.
◆ Relaxing haven to unwind away from the stresses and strains of work.
◆ Low-maintenance garden means less time having to garden and more time enjoying the garden and other hobbies/interests.

It's important to see selling as not only a necessary function, but also an enjoyable one. There is no reason why you should shy away from it. Naturally, the more you do, the better you become. Before any sales appointment, make sure that you are prepared:

◆ Prepare for the likely questions you will be asked. You'll get a good idea of what your prospective client wants of you during the initial telephone discussion.

◆ Make sure that you are in a positive frame of mind. Nothing is worse than having someone call to give you an estimate who moans about the weather, football results, interest rates and the like. People want somebody positive and enthusiastic to arrive at their doorstep and tell them they can create the garden of their dreams at an affordable price.

◆ Have with you or at least in your vehicle photographs of previous work.

◆ You'll also need to have available: 10m and 30m measuring tapes, pencil, notepad, ruler and clipboard to write on.

Successful selling is largely a result of careful preparation, knowing your subject and not being afraid to tell someone how much it's going to cost, and once this is done, asking for the order.

Help Directory

Further education

Colleges offering correspondence courses

The Horticultural Correspondence College
Freepost 9GW, Chippenham SN15 2BR
Tel: 0800 378918

The Institute for Horticultural and Rural Studies
Cranmere Road, Okehampton, Devon EX20 1UE
Tel: 01837 659600

ICS
International Correspondence Schools, Freepost 882, 8 Elliot Place, Clydeway, Glasgow,
G3 8BR
Tel: 01 285 2533

KLC School of Interior and Garden Design
Unit 503, The Chambers, Chelsea Harbour, London SW10 OXF

The Institute of Garden Design
Tel: 01934 713 563

Extended Learning Opportunities
4 Highlands Road, Hadleigh, Suffolk 1P7 5HU
Tel: 01437 828796

Individual Learning Account (ILA)
Tel: 0800 100 901

Tool and equipment suppliers (mail order)

Northern Tool and Equipment Co (UK) Ltd
Tel: 0800 169 2266
www.northerntooluk.com

Societies and agencies

Countryside Agency Head Office
John Dower House, Crescent Place, Cheltenham, Gloucestershire GL50 3RA
Tel: 01242 5211381

RHS – Royal Horticultural Society
RHS Information, PO Box 313, London SW1P 2PE
Tel: 0845 130 4646

Help with your business

Federation of Small Businesses
Whittle Way, Blackpool Business Park, Blackpool, Lancs FY4 2FE
Tel: 01253 336000

Women into Business
Curzon House, Church Road, Windlesham, Surrey GU20 6BH
Tel: 01276 452010

Lawyers for Your Business
Helpline: 020 7405 9075

The Inland Revenue New Enterprise Support Initiative
Tel: 0845 607 0143

The Institute of Small Business Advisors
Response House, Queens Street North, Chesterfield S41 9AU

Tel: 01246 453322

The Enterprise Centre
www.enterprise-centre.co.uk

Web sites

Carry on Gardening www.carryongardening.org.uk
Help site with award winning forum.

Gardening UK www.gardening-uk.co.uk
Information site on products, supplies, news and features

Lets Go Gardening www.letsgogardening.co.uk
Shopping and information site with clubs and societies.

BBC – Gardening www.bbc.co.uk/gardening
Useful site for inspiration on design work with lots of information and gardening craft.

Gardening Links www.gardenlinks.ndo.co.uk
Directory site for UK gardening and gardens.

The Royal Horticultural Society www.rhs.org.uk
Essential reading for every professional gardener.

Landscape Planner
UK directory of landscapers and garden designers.

Index

accidents, 43, 57, 194
advertising, 15, 131, 135, 136, 145–148
aeration, 109
annual tax return, 159, 169, 180
autumn, 188

banks, 140–143
bookkeeping, 69, 164–169
business planning, 20–29, 208
business stationery, 234

capital, 20, 32, 78, 79, 84
cash flow, 35, 38, 87
catalogue selling, 115
churches, 6
client records, 61
coaching, 16, 75
commercial market, 6
complaints handling, 203
contingency planning, 43
costs, 53
craft fairs, 152

debt recovery, 170–173
diary, 64, 67, 192
difficult people, 202
directories, 154
DIY, 112
domestic market, 5

earnings, 25, 27
economies of scale, 65
estate agents, 6
estimates, 90, 94
exhibitions, 152
expenditure, 159, 166

family/personal problems, 200, 201
financial health, 26
financing, 32, 87, 88
first aid, 200
full-time work, 4, 14

garden design, 74, 75
garden planning, 74, 75
gardening round, 51
guesthouses, 6

hiring machinery, 80
home-based nursery, 115

image, 129, 133
income, 166
Inland Revenue, 164–169
input tax, 163
insurance, 38, 44, 56, 86
internet, 212
invoices, 167, 168

late payers, 170

lawn-cutting, 109, 182–189

legal action, 171, 206

letterhead, 140

limited company, 34

local authority, 6

manual systems, 61, 165

market research, 9, 17

marketing, 89

minimum charge, 65

National Insurance Contributions, 161

net profit, 40

output tax, 163

partnership, 34, 160

part-time work, 4, 13, 28, 52, 211

PAYE, 160

payment terms, 169

personal computers, 60

positive cash flow, 87

premises, 100

press interest, 152

pricing, 58, 98

profit and loss, 40

property management, 6

protective clothing, 200

quotes, 90

receipts, 36, 167

research methods, 122

residents' associations, 6

sales, 137, 149, 167, 213–220

scarification, 181, 189

schools, 6

self-employed, 4, 11, 161, 196

self profile, 10, 48

skills analysis, 7

software, 165

sole trader, 34, 161

spin-offs, 106

spring, 181–182

staff, 173–176

start-up costs, 31, 79

strategy, 24, 202

stress, 195

summer, 185, 186

survival income, 27

surveys, 63

tax, 162, 180

telephone lines, 31

tools, 29, 30, 54, 79, 81

trading profit, 40

tree surgery, 74

VAT, 163–164

vehicles, 84

waste, disposing of, 55

weather, 177, 197

web sites, 157

weed killers, 200

winter, 190–192

working capital, 78